Exalt Thyself as the Eagle

A Prophetic call to Turn this Nation Around

BY

Dennis James Woods

Exalt Thyself as the Eagle:
A Prophetic Call to Turn this Nation Around

ISBN-13: 978-1-939654-65-6
ISBN-10: 1939654653

Printed in the United States
10 9 8 7 6 5 4 3 2 1

Cover design by: Legacy Design Inc
Legacydesigninc@gmail.com

Published by
Life To Legacy, LLC
P.O. Box 57
Blue Island, IL 60406
877-267-7477
www.Life2Legacy.com
Life2legacybooks@att.net

Contents

Introduction 5

1 Rightly Dividing the Word of Prophecy 17

2 The Prophecy of Obadiah 27

3 The United States-Israel's Big Brother 53

4 America In Decline 61

5 Thou Are Greatly Despised 95

6 The Pride of Your Heart has Deceived You 109

7 Dwelling in the Clefts of the Rocks 119

8 Exalt Thyself as the Eagle 127

9 A Nest Among the Stars 135

10 As You Have Done-
it Shall be Done to You 143

11 Turn this Nation Around 157

About the Author 175

Endnotes 177

Introduction

During the Bicentennial celebration of 1976, one of America's celebrated R&B artists, the late, great Ray Charles, offered up a soulful rendition of a patriotic song titled "America the Beautiful." Though Charles' inspiring version of this song was a departure from the more formal arrangement, it captured the hearts and souls of countless Americans and is among Charles' most cherished performances. Interestingly, "America the Beautiful" was not originally written as a song but originated from a poem, written and published by Katharine Lee Bates in 1895, titled "Pikes Peak." It was years later when it was musically arranged by Samuel A. Ward, and in 1910, was subsequently published as "America the Beautiful."

Arguably one of the greatest national songs ever written, in the early 1960s there was a move to have this song receive legal status as a national hymn or anthem, but this effort failed to come to fruition. Although the song never received such legal status, it never lost its prominent place in the annals of American musical history and to this day is sung at political, sports, and national events alike. The opening verse of this inspiring song reads as follows:

O beautiful for spacious skies, for amber waves of grain. For purple mountain majesties, above the fruited plain! America! America! God shed His grace on thee, and crown thy good with brotherhood from sea to shining sea!

The first verse of this song encapsulates the unparalleled

majesty and blessedness that America has enjoyed for decades. Clearly, America was and is the enviable beneficiary of God's grace, the foundation of her prosperity, prestige, power, and national pride. In his debut book titled *Project America*, Dr. Marshall Hatch, in the "Prelude," observes the following:

> The American Project is the ongoing experiment with a unique form of democracy that values equality of opportunity for every person above all else. That is an amazing ideal. The founding document of the Republic enshrined a divine mandate to honor the sacredness of human potential in every individual person. The heart of this principle presupposes political rights and economic self-determination. The possibility of upward mobility, the blessings of liberty, and the pursuit of happiness emerged from a new world with new possibilities.[1]

Here, Dr. Hatch observes that America was a unique form of democracy, unique in that she "values equality of opportunity for every person above all else." On the surface, this altruistic yet lofty principle seems to offer a roadmap to success for anyone in the pursuit of happiness. It was this very principle that drew millions of immigrants mostly from Europe to come to the fertile shores of America in search of religious and political freedom. On the other hand, hundreds of thousands of Africans came bound in chains under the cruel, oppressing burden of chattel slavery. Yet each soul, whether willingly or unwillingly, stepped upon the stage of one of the greatest empires that the world has ever known. The question is, why? Why were those who came to America, whether bond or free, chosen to be a part of this American experiment?

An answer to this great question is found in Acts 17, where observations are made by the apostle Paul in an arena called the Areopagus also known as "Mars Hill." *The New Living Translation* emphasizes a portion of Paul's compelling argument to the Greek philosophers this way:

> From one man he created all the nations throughout the whole earth. He decided beforehand when they should rise and fall, and he determined their boundaries. His purpose was for the nations to seek after God and perhaps feel their way toward him and find him—though he is not far from any one of us. For in him we live and move and exist. As some of your own poets have said, "We are his offspring."
>
> Acts 17:26-28

Through the wisdom of the Holy Spirit, Paul employs great apologetic skill as he addresses the typical Platonic worldview, which was popular philosophy of that day, to draw their attention to a theistic biblical worldview, emphasizing God's complete providential control over all humankind. Speaking of the people of the world, Paul states that God "decided beforehand when they should rise and fall, and he determined their boundaries." Clearly, Paul is emphasizing God's complete sovereign control over the entire human race and the nations where they would dwell. As the apostle asserts, "His purpose was for the nations to seek after God and perhaps feel their way toward him and find him."

God had a purpose for each person who was a partaker of

the American experiment. In His purpose was the power to bring about His plan for the nations, where men would seek after Him in faith and love, and reverence Him as the sovereign God. As Paul went on to say, "…in him, we live, move and have our being." Though men like to see themselves as being the captain of their own soul, it is God who is truly in control.

A sobering example of God's total control over the nations is found in the book of Daniel: King Nebuchadnezzar, the great Babylonian king, who in his arrogance and pride sought to defy God after He warned him not to do so. The foolish king refused to submit. Therefore, God responded to Nebuchadnezzar's insolence by taking his throne and giving it to another. He added insult to injury by giving Nebuchadnezzar the mind of a wild animal for seven long years, where he lived in the wilderness and ate grass like an ox. The Bible also informs us that Nebuchadnezzar's hair grew out like an eagle's feathers and his nails grew long like bird claws. After the seven years had passed, God had finished making His point, and restored Nebuchadnezzar to his former glory. It is from this perspective that Nebuchadnezzar makes the following observation:

> …I, Nebuchadnezzar, raised my eyes toward heaven, and my sanity was restored. Then I praised the Most High; I honored and glorified him who lives forever. His dominion is an eternal dominion; his kingdom endures from generation to generation. All the peoples of the earth are regarded as nothing. He does as he pleases with the powers of heaven and the peoples of the earth. No one can

hold back his hand or say to him: "What have you done?"
Daniel 4:34-35, NIV 2011

It is simply best that we understand what David also concluded: "The earth is the LORD's, and everything in it, the world, and all who live in it..." (Psalm 24:1, NIV 2011).

As we continue the discussion about the peoples and nations of the world, many of the nations around today have roots that go back to biblical times. For example, Nebuchadnezzar's Babylon is today's modern-day Iraq, where the ruins of the ancient city are about 70 miles south of modern-day Baghdad. The Bible also provides references to African nations like Egypt, Libya, and Ethiopia; each of these nations is still among the global community today. The same is true of European nations like Greece, Rome, Italy, and Spain. Modern-day Asian nations are referred to as the "kings of the East." Ancient cities like Ephesus located in Asia Minor, now modern-day Turkey, attract tourists from all over the world. Middle Eastern nations such as Israel, Syria, Lebanon, Jordan, Persia (Iran), and Babylon (Iraq) are all subjects of biblical scrutiny. The kings of the upper north, such as Russia and Eastern European nations, are mentioned, while vague references to the uttermost parts (or ends) of the earth seem to encompass nations, isles, and kingdoms far beyond the known world during biblical times. Great empires such as the Egyptian, Assyrian, Babylonian, Medo-Persian, Grecian, Syrian, and Roman Empires are all found in the Scriptures.

This leads to a greater question: "Where is America in the Scriptures?" America has played a key role in revolutionizing the entire world through her economic and industrial influence. She has changed the course of the world through her military influence, changed how the global civilizations function through her innovations and inventions, and even played a crucial role in the re-establishment of the Jewish nation, Israel. From the Industrial Revolution of the late nineteenth century to World War II, America was catapulted into world dominance, and in many ways is still a leader among the nations today.

Such unparalleled prominence has caused many to wonder why America is not in the Bible. The Bible clearly mentions future times in the numerous end-time prophetic scenarios where many nations are explicitly identified. As I am writing this book in 2015, President Barack Obama is fighting feverishly, along with Secretary of State John Kerry, to pass a nuclear arms agreement with the nation of Iran that would permit Iran to pursue nuclear research and development for peaceful purposes but stop its development of nuclear weapons. Ironically, Iran is identified as one of the nations that will invade Israel along with a host of countries headed up by Russia (Gog and Magog, cf. Ezekiel 38-39). Iran, along with all the other nations named in Ezekiel, has an appointed day in future prophetic destiny. Nevertheless, where is the United States?

The United States is one of the few world superpowers. According to the *American Heritage Dictionary*, a *super-*

power is "A powerful and influential nation, especially a nuclear power that dominates its allies or client states in an international power bloc." Of the world's superpowers like Russia, China, and Great Britain, the United States has been the leader of them all and is the dominant military power in the world, with a vast, highly diversified, technically advanced military, and enough nuclear weaponry to destroy the world many times over.

Economically, America is also a dominating force in global economics (although this is rapidly shifting). It is the principal member of the G-20, the twenty great economic powers of the world. This group consists of the finance ministers and central bank governors of the twenty major advanced economies as reported by the International Monetary Fund. The members of this group which includes Canada, France, Germany, Italy, Japan, the United Kingdom, United States and the European Union, meet primarily to discuss economic issues that affect global financial governance and international monetary control and regulations.

The American dollar is a dominant world currency and is one of the world's reserve currencies. A *reserve currency* is held in significant quantities by governments and institutions as part of their foreign exchange reserves. The reserve currency is commonly used in international transactions and often considered a hard currency and/or "safe-haven" currency. Citizens of a country that issues a reserve currency can purchase imports and borrow across international borders more cheaply than people in other nations, because they don't need to exchange their currency to do so. Important international resources, such as oil and gold, are all traded in American dollars. This, along with American's enormous industrial complex and gross national product, keeps the United States at the top of the heap among the economic powers of the world.

Though relatively young, America also holds enormous influence in the geopolitical realm by negotiating international treaties, establishing and backing foreign governments, and through monetary and political support. America, with its huge military machine, flexes her muscles by having military bases all over the world (without any foreign military bases being in America). She is the largest exporter of military armament to a host of nations around the world. To the chagrin of many, both foreign and national, America acts as the world police, enforcing "freedom" and protecting America's and its allies' interests.

America, being on a land mass with two great oceans on either shore, would make an invasion extremely difficult. The fact that she is rich with natural resources such as oil, coal, natural gas, and steel makes her less vulnerable to foreign nations. With the vast Great Plains to support the world's largest agricultural complex, she is the number one exporter of agricultural products in the world. America has been divinely positioned to enjoy privilege, prestige, and power like no other nation before her.

As quoted earlier, Dr. Hatch, speaking of America, so

eloquently states, "The heart of this principle presupposes political rights and economic self-determination. The possibility of upward mobility, the blessings of liberty, and the pursuit of happiness emerged from a new world with new possibilities." From the pages of her founding document, America offered freedoms and liberties that no other nation in the world has ever offered, a democratic government with political and religious freedom all guaranteed to its citizenry by way of its Constitution and Bill of Rights.

Though some of the signers of the Declaration of Independence were not Christians, many were, and the values that they held so dear were etched into the cornerstone of this great country when they formed this republic. Therefore, many of our laws reflect Judeo-Christian principles, and there was an obvious reverence and respect for the theistic God of the Bible, the Creator of the universe. This is evident among the opening words of the Declaration of Independence:

> We hold these truths to be self-evident, that all men are created equal, that they are endowed by their Creator with certain unalienable Rights, that among these are Life, Liberty and the pursuit of Happiness.

It is important to note that these founding words did not say that all men "evolved through natural selection." It doesn't say that the "universe" endowed us with inalienable rights resulting from the "big bang." No, the operative words here are *Creator* and *created*. Obviously, anything created has to have a creator, as it emphatically states in Genesis 1:1: "In the beginning God created the heavens and the earth...." Clearly, the God of the Bible was the Creator that the founding fathers had in mind when the Declaration of Independence was written.

In my opinion, which is shared by millions of Americans, America, though far from perfect, was founded upon biblical principles and reverence to the God of the Bible. Therefore, the national motto adopted in 1957, "In God We Trust," was actually printed on coins as early as 1864. Though not going as far as to directly quote the Bible, the motto "In God We Trust" clearly set America apart from nations such as the Soviet Union that embraced a form of state atheism. At one time in our history, America was proud to embrace the God of the Bible. Hence the lyrics of "America the Beautiful": *America! America! God shed His grace on thee, and crown thy good with brotherhood from sea to shining sea.* At one point America led the world in science and innovation, industry, opportunity, and education, but now has fallen behind in just about every category.

America no longer wants to be "one nation under God" as affirmed in the Pledge of Allegiance. America wants to be one nation "away" from God. America has strayed far away from a nation that celebrated its *freedom of religion* and the role that the Church has played in forging this great republic. She has now given way to a secular humanist agenda of *freedom from religion* that recoils at the very mention of God.

It is for this very reason that I write this book. This book is a prophetic warning to our great nation, America, whose power and glory are quickly fading. The Bible warns, "The wicked shall be turned into hell, *And* all the nations that forget God" (Psalm 9:17, NKJV). The *New Living Translation* gives this perspective: "The wicked will go down to the grave. This is the fate of all the nations who ignore God." This prophetic warning applies to all the nations who *forget* or *ignore* God, and therefore certainly applies to the United States, who not only *ignores* and *forgets,* but openly *defies* God.

This book is a clarion call, a prophetic warning that in the midst of all our wealth, technology, military prowess, and political and economic power, America is rotting from within, morally bankrupt, and headed for destruction. Why do I believe that America is headed for destruction? The answer is found in a passage of Scripture from an obscure and enigmatic prophet by the name of Obadiah. A discussion of the historicity of Obadiah the prophet himself and his prophecy along with the introduction and exposition of the thematic text will be examined throughout subsequent chapters of this book.

Chapter 1
Rightly Dividing the Word of Prophecy

Before we can fully immerse ourselves in this study, it is necessary to cover some of the basic rules of interpreting prophecy. Without these rules, prophecy quickly downgrades to "private interpretation." The science of biblical interpretation called *hermeneutics* is where we get the rules for how we should interpret the Scriptures. One of these rules is that Scriptures are to be interpreted according to their *grammatical-historical* context, and should only be understood within the scope of what the author intended. This fundamental rule acts as a guideline to keep us from ending up in left field and reaching an erroneous interpretation. As the Bible declares, "All Scripture *is* given by inspiration of God, and *is* profitable for doctrine, for reproof, for correction, for instruction in righteousness, that the man of God may be complete, thoroughly equipped for every good work" (2 Timothy 3:16-17, NKJV). Since we understand that Scripture is given by divine inspiration, we can trust that it is infallible, because the God from which it came is infallible.

Another important principle found in Scripture concerning the veracity of prophecy is found in 2 Peter 1:20-21 where the Scripture declares, "knowing this first, that no prophecy of Scripture is of any private interpretation, for prophecy never came by the will of man, but holy men of God spoke *as they were* moved by the Holy Spirit." (NKJV) Since God is the source of Scripture, that means we are getting God's perspective on human matters in accordance with the dictates of His own purpose and will.

Since God is eternal, omniscient, omnipotent, and omnipresent, He is all knowing, all powerful, and fills all time and space. Only He can reveal future events in such detail that allows us to read them as if they were history. For example, there are several prophecies found in the book of Revelation that have not yet occurred, such as the binding of Satan and his incarceration in the abyss (Revelation 20:1-3). Yet we read about this future event as though it had already occurred because we are getting God's perspective, which is not limited by time or space, and who is already in the future. In a sense, it is like having prophetic hindsight. Through prophecy, we can evaluate a future event and benefit by knowing what is to come, while at the same time read it as if those future events have already happened. In other words, we know what is coming before it gets here. However, God is not merely predicting the future as a weatherman would predict without certainty or having control over the predicted weather events. No, God foreknows, elects, and predestinates, and has the power to bring everything to pass according to His own will (Acts 15:18, Isaiah: 42.9).

With these basic concepts in mind, let us begin our study of rightly dividing the word of prophecy.

1. A prophecy may appear as one event, but in reality, there may be one, two, three or even fourfold fulfillment.

2. A prophecy may be fulfilled shortly after its delivery or at a much later date.

3. Prophecy can be ethically conditioned, which means some of the conditions of the prophecy are based upon the behavior of the recipient, and can be recalled.

4. Many prophecies are fulfilled literally, such as prophecies concerning Christ.

5. The form and character of prophecy are conditioned by the times of the writer and will describe a future event in language and imagery familiar with his present-day reality. John, in writing Revelation, could not have known what a mechanized army and modern weaponry were, but he used descriptive language such as horses, horsemen, and breastplates of fire (e.g. Revelation 9:16-19).

6. The prophet may see things together that are actually far apart. In Daniel 12:2, Daniel sees both resurrections, and Jesus characterizes both resurrections in one view (John 5:29), but both are actually separated by one thousand years (Revelation 20:4-6).

7. Prophecies frequently form parts of a whole and must be considered and compared to other prophecies. For example, interpreting the prophecies in the book of Revelation

require an understanding of the prophecies of Daniel.

8. As it relates to the time element of prophecy, when the time of fulfillment of a prophecy was not revealed, the prophet saw those prophecies as continuous. They saw the future in terms of space, not in time. The whole, therefore, appears foreshortened, in perspective, rather than actual distance. From our perspective on earth, we group stars together as little white dots that can be connected to form certain imagery because they appear as if they are on a dark, two-dimensional tapestry. However, in reality those same stars may be thousands or millions of light-years apart. Therefore, it is doubtful that any of the prophets or apostles had an inkling of how much time would lapse before the fulfillment of the things about which they wrote.

9. The prophets were the vessels that God used to communicate prophecy, but in many instances they did not understand the very things they were writing. They neither fully understood the purpose of prophecy nor when it would be fulfilled. God reveals prophecy on a need-to-know basis. He may hold back understanding from the prophet, but open up understanding to whom the prophecy applies, which, in some cases, may be thousands of years later. For example, Daniel stated, "Although I heard, I did not understand. Then I said, 'My lord, what *shall be* the end of these *things*?' And he said, 'Go *your way*, Daniel, for the words *are* closed up and sealed till the time of the end'" (Daniel 12:8-9, NKJV).

Also, in the book of Acts we find this passage: "Therefore, when they had come together, they asked Him, saying, 'Lord, will You at this time restore the kingdom to Israel?' And He said to them, it is not for you to know times or seasons which the Father has put in His own authority'" (Acts 1:6-7, NKJV). In Revelation 10:4, John was about to write the utterances of the *seven thunders*, but was told not to write them down. Here is a clear example of God letting us know that He intentionally does not reveal everything. From this, we may conclude that the book of Revelation itself is incomplete, because the Bible explicitly states that John was prohibited from sharing what he heard the seven thunders say. Therefore, in Revelation we have the messages to the seven churches, the seven seals, the seven trumpets, the seven thunders (redacted), and the seven bowls. It is beyond the ability of even human speculation what information about the future was contained in the words of the seven thunders, except to know that God wanted those words specifically kept secret.

The Interpretation of Figurative Language

Another complexity of interpreting prophecy is knowing when to interpret prophecy literary or figuratively. A succinct rule put forth by David L. Cooper states the following:

> When the plain sense of the Scripture makes common sense, seek no other sense; therefore, take every word at its primary, ordinary, usual, literal meaning unless the facts of the immediate context, studied in the light of related passages and axiomatic and fundamental truths, indicate clearly otherwise.[2]

In the Gospel narrative, Jesus often spoke of Himself figuratively. At one point, His use of figurative language caused some of His disciples to stop following Him. In John, Jesus states:

> "Whoever eats My flesh and drinks My blood has eternal life, and I will raise him up at the last day"...Therefore many of His disciples, when they heard *this*, said, "This is a hard saying; who can understand it?"...From that *time* many of His disciples went back and walked with Him no more.
>
> John 6:54, 60, 66, NKJV

Here we have an example of how individuals can trip up on literally interpreting figurative language. Clearly the meaning of the figurative language is what was important, not the figurative language itself. The Lord was not suggesting that the disciples should resort to cannibalism (eating his flesh) or become *hematophagous*, blood-feeding creatures. That is clearly beyond the common-sense meaning of what Jesus was saying. The result of taking the figurative language literally caused a serious misunderstanding of Jesus' sacrificial, redemptive message and caused these "other" disciples to follow Him no more.

Here are some basic rules in determining whether a passage should be interpreted literally or figuratively. The approach should be to interpret passages of Scripture literally unless:

a. the Scripture obviously contains figurative language.

b. the New Testament gives authority to interpreting the passage other than literally.

c. the literal interpretation would produce a contradiction of truths, facts, biblical principles, or lead to an absurdity.

d. a choice is made to interpret the figurative by the didactic. Obscure Old Testament passages should be interpreted in the light of New Testament revelation, not the other way around.

e. a decision has been made to accept the clear and plain parts of Scripture as the basis for getting a true meaning of the more difficult parts of Scripture.

The Law of Double Reference

Among the laws of interpreting prophecy, few are as important as the Law of Double Reference. Basically, the Law of Double Reference helps us understand an important principle about interpreting prophecy, which is that one prophecy may focus on two different events separated by a vast amount of time as to their fulfillment. Often God gave a message for the prophet's day, as well as had a prophecy for a future time. In this prophetic manner, God gave the near and far views so that the fulfillment of one should be the assurance of the fulfillment of the other. For example, in Daniel 11, we get the history (still future of Daniel's time) of Antiochus Epiphanes, who desecrated the Jewish temple in 167 B.C., when he sacrificed a pig on the altar and then erected a statue of Zeus. This was an "abomination of desolation." This desecration of the temple led to the Maccabean Revolt, led by Judas Maccabeus.

It was during this revolt that the Jewish holiday Hanukkah was birthed. In *The Bible Knowledge Commentary*, Dr. Walvoord, speaking of Daniel 11, asserts:

> In verses 36-45 a leader is described who is introduced simply as "the king." Some suggest that this is Antiochus IV Epiphanes and that the verses describe additional incursions of his into Israel. However, the details given in these verses were not fulfilled by Antiochus. True, Antiochus was a foreshadowing of a king who will come…but the two are not the same. One is past, and the other is future.[3]

Antiochus' actions were the foreshadowing of a greater event of the same nature to be fulfilled by the Antichrist. In His Mount Olivet discourse, Jesus referred to Daniel's prophecy, which spoke of a greater fulfillment of the historical desecration committed by Antiochus, when He stated:

> So when you see standing in the holy place 'the abomination that causes desolation,' spoken of through the prophet Daniel—let the reader understand—then let those who are in Judea flee to the mountains. Let no one on the housetop go down to take anything out of the house. Let no one in the field go back to get their cloak. For then there will be great distress, unequaled from the beginning of the world until now—and never to be equaled again.
>
> Matthew 24:15-18, 21, NIV 2011

Here there is a double reference to antiquity and yet another to the future. Just as Antiochus erected the image of Zeus in the holy place, so shall the Antichrist enter the rebuilt temple and erect his own image, claiming himself to be God (2 Thessalonians 2:4, Revelation 13:14-15). Jesus is referencing both events—one in the past, the other one in the future.

When considering the importance of the Law of Double Reference, understand that the same prophecies have a double meaning and refer to different events: one near, the other one far. The scope of the prophecy could have several events in view, whether or not the prophet himself understood it that way. The context of the prophecy could be applicable to one and partly to another—a transition that is not always easily distinguishable. However, what has not been fulfilled in one can find future fulfillment in another, and what has already been fulfilled can be the basis for expecting what is yet to be fulfilled.

CHAPTER 2
THE PROPHECY OF OBADIAH

Behold, I have made thee small among the heathen: thou art greatly despised. The pride of thine heart hath deceived thee, thou that dwellest in the clefts of the rock, whose habitation *is* high; that saith in his heart, Who shall bring me down to the ground? Though thou *exalt* thyself as the eagle, and though thou set thy nest among the stars, thence will I bring thee down, saith the LORD.
Obadiah 1:2-4, KJV

The day of the LORD is near for all nations. As you have done, it will be done to you; your deeds will return upon your own head. Just as you drank on my holy hill, so all the nations will drink continually; they will drink and drink and be as if they had never been.
Obadiah 1:15-16, NIV

If one were to conduct a cursory reading of the above passages, it may not be apparent that this ancient prophecy could contain information about a powerful nation of the twenty-first century. However, you will discover that the characteristics of a great modern nation have been hiding in plain sight within the text of this prophecy. What I am proposing in this book is indeed both shocking and controversial. Historically, Obadiah is writing a prophecy concerning the destruction of the ancient Edomites, who at the time of this prophecy lived in a naturally fortified rocky territory full of mountains and plateaus. The primary city of these ancient people, which was also the focus of their national pride, was later to be called Petra. However, the intriguing aspect of this prophecy also looks forward to an eschatological event called "the day of the Lord." It is that day on which much end-time prophecy is focused and culminates with the Lord's return to establish His millennial reign here on earth. Since Obadiah also prophesied about the day of the Lord, his prophecy is not solely historical but futuristic as well.

The ancient Edomites possessed territory in the region of the Middle East known today as Jordan. However, this ancient civilization has long been off the scene as a nation in the territory that they once occupied. Yet Obadiah's prophecy extends all the way into the time of the end. It is unlikely that the modern-day Jordanians fit this prophecy, nor is it tenable to claim that they are the same people as the Edomites of old. It is also not reasonable to expect a resurgence of the ancient city of Petra, rising from the ashes of millennia past. So then, in its end-time focus, to whom was this prophecy written? I emphasize, it cannot be the ancient Edomites! This book seeks to answer that perplexing question. It is also the premise of this book to show the uncanny parallels between God's characterization of the ancient Edomites and how closely it resembles the United States of America. However, before we go deeper into this study, we must first start building from a grammatical-historical foundation.

The Prophet and the Book of Obadiah

The name Obadiah was a common name during Old Testament times. Thirteen individuals bore the name Obadiah, the prophet being one of them. However, nothing is known about this enigmatic prophet. His name, however, means either "worshiper of Jehovah"[4] or "serving Jah."[5] Obadiah is the shortest book of the Old Testament, having only twenty-one verses. The purpose of the book is twofold: a) to delineate God's judgment of Edom for its lack of brotherly concern for Judah, and b) to set forth a final triumph in the day of the Lord.[6] Adding to its obscurity, Obadiah is a prophetic book that is not quoted anywhere in the New Testament, but shares notable commonalities with the prophet Jeremiah. Obadiah 1-9 is amazingly close to Jeremiah 49:7-22. Because of this, some theorize that either Obadiah borrowed from Jeremiah or vice versa. The possibility also exists that both prophets shared a common source in regards to the stated verses. However, none are certain about these possibilities.

Esau and Edomites

The Edomites are the descendants of Esau, who was the eldest son of Isaac and Rebecca, and twin brother of Jacob. From the very beginning, these brothers had a turbulent co-existence that began in their mother's womb. While Rebecca was pregnant with these twins, she began experiencing so much commotion between the two boys that she prayed to God for an answer. In Genesis 25, we find the circumstances surrounding Esau and Jacob's birth, and the reason for their prenatal conflict:

> Now Isaac pleaded with the Lord for his wife, because she *was* barren; and the Lord granted his plea, and Rebekah his wife conceived. But the children struggled together within her; and she said, "If *all is* well, why *am I like* this?" So she went to inquire of the Lord. And the Lord said to her: "Two nations *are* in your womb, Two peoples shall be separated from your body; *One* people shall be stronger than the other, And the older shall serve the younger." So when her days were fulfilled *for her* to give birth, indeed *there were* twins in her womb. And the first came out red. *He was* like a hairy garment all over; so they called his name Esau.
>
> Genesis 25:21-25, NKJV

In this passage, we have God's election at work, a subject that Paul emphasizes in Romans 9. The issue of election is significant because God chose Jacob to be over Esau. This went against Hebrew customs, where the eldest son was to receive the double-portion of the blessing and the birthright. However, before these boys were even born, so that God's election might stand, God determined that the older, Esau, shall serve the younger, Jacob.

The name *Esau* means "hairy."[7] Esau was favored by Isaac because he was an outdoorsman and a skilled hunter, and he could cook Isaac's favorite meal, "the savory venison meat," whereas Jacob, favored by his mother Rebecca, was a "plain" man that dwelt in the tents. The contentions between the two brothers in the womb turned out to be prophetic in that there were sharp contentions between the two in adult life, which would be the basis for generational contentions among their respective tribes long after the progenitors were dead.

Esau Sells his Birthright

There were two significant transactions between the two brothers that had a great impact on their relationship and destiny. The first was when Jacob exploited Esau when he was hungry:

> Now Jacob cooked a stew; and Esau came in from the field, and he *was* weary. And Esau said to Jacob, "Please feed me with that same red *stew*, for I *am* weary." Therefore his name was called Edom. But Jacob said, "Sell me your birthright as of this day." And Esau said, "Look, I *am* about to die; so what *is* this birthright to me?" Then Jacob said, "Swear to me as of this day." So he swore to him, and sold his birthright to Jacob. And Jacob gave Esau bread and stew of lentils; then he ate and drank, arose, and went his way. Thus Esau despised *his* birthright.
>
> Genesis 25:29-34, NKJV

Here we have the account of Esau selling his birthright. The *birthright* was the status of firstborn: it meant the headship of the family and a double share of the estate.[8] After coming back from a long day in the field, Esau said, "I am so hungry that I am starving to death." Jacob, whose name means "heel catcher"[9] (a Hebrew idiom for supplanter or deceiver), saw an opportunity to exploit his brother's weakness and proposed selling his birthright for some of Jacob's red soup (thus the name *Edom*, meaning "red," see Genesis 25:31). Esau's response to Jacob was, "I *am* about to die; so what *is* this birthright to me…Esau despised *his* birthright." The word *despise* comes from the Hebrew word *bāzâ*, which means "to disesteem or to disdain."[10] Therefore, Esau's desires came from a mindset of immediate self-gratification…a carnal spirit preferring temporal self-serving material interest over spiritual things. Clearly, the birthright belonged to Esau, but he *chose* to sell it. As a result, Esau's choice changed his destiny. He thought so trivially of his birthright that he sold it for a bowl of red soup, which is tantamount to utter contempt for the things of God. This is a dominant characteristic of the Edomite people and nation, whose very name traces back to Esau's contempt for his own position in God. In Hebrews, the Bible, speaking of Esau, states:

> See that no one is sexually immoral, or is godless like Esau, who for a single meal sold his inheritance rights as the oldest son. Afterward, as you know, when he wanted to inherit this blessing, he was rejected. Even though he sought the blessing with tears, he could not change what he had done.
>
> Hebrews 12:16-17, NIV

Esau's despising of his birthright is tantamount to being "godless" or, as the *King James Version* says, a "profane person." The synonyms for profane are irreverent, irreligious, blasphemous, sacrilegious, wicked, and disrespectful. These are some of the characteristics of the Edomites, who had a long history of being enemies of Jacob's (Israel's) descendants.

Jacob Steals the Blessing

The second transaction is where Jacob (the supplanter), in collusion with his mother Rebecca, swindles the blessing by having Jacob pose as his brother Esau. They both took advantage of the fact that Isaac was in poor health, blind, and near death. When Isaac requested that Esau go catch and prepare his favorite meal, Rebecca and Jacob sprang into action. Rebecca prepared the savory venison, and Jacob put on Esau's clothes in order to smell like his brother. In order to feel like Esau, Rebecca also prepared goatskin to put on his arms and neck, to imitate Esau's rugged, hairy body.

Though Isaac was old and sick, he was not a fool, and immediately became suspicious because Jacob returned too quickly with the meal. Secondly, though Jacob had on a disguise, he could not imitate Esau's voice. Isaac was perplexed because he knew it was Jacob's voice he heard, so he wanted to feel and smell him. The disguise worked. With his initial suspicion arrested, he proceeded to bless Jacob, believing it was Esau. The blessing follows:

> And he came near and kissed him; and he smelled the smell of his clothing, and blessed him and said: "Surely, the smell of my son *Is* like the smell of a field Which the Lord has blessed. Therefore may God give you Of the dew of heaven, Of the fatness of the earth, And plenty of grain and wine. Let peoples serve you, And nations bow down to you. Be master over your brethren, And let your mother's sons bow down to you. Cursed *be* everyone who curses you, And blessed *be* those who bless you!"
>
> Genesis 27:27-29, NKJV

Now that the blessing had been given to Jacob, it could not be reversed or rescinded. When Esau returned from the field, he found out what his brother had done. Esau begged Isaac to bless him too, but it was too late. The preferred blessing had already been given. Esau and his people would be subservient to Jacob and his offspring. For this swindling act, Esau vowed to kill his brother (Genesis 27:34-41). With no more blessings to bequeath, these are the words that Isaac spoke over Esau, which amounts to a blessing in reverse.

> Esau said to his father, "Do you have only one blessing, my father? Bless me too, my father!" Then Esau wept aloud. His father Isaac answered him, "Your dwelling will be away from the earth's richness, away from the dew of heaven above. You will live by the sword and you will serve your brother. But when you grow restless, you will throw his yoke from off your neck."
>
> Genesis 27:38-40, NIV

From this passage, we find that the Edomites would be a people of the sword, who would not be blessed the same as Israel, but yet they would be their own nation. Everything that they had would come by the sword. This implies a violent, warlike people that use their sword (weapons) to take from others what is not theirs. And when coupled with being profane, meaning irreverent, irreligious, blasphemous, sacrilegious, wicked, disrespectful, and godless, this is a potent mixture for a volatile society headed for destruction. Though Isaac pronounced that Edom was to serve Israel, he also predicted that they would be powerful and gain dominion. "...It shall come to pass when thou shalt have the dominion, that thou shalt break his yoke from off thy neck" (Genesis 27:40, KJV). Therefore, the Edomites were not always subservient to Israel but became a thriving society centuries later.

Before being destroyed by the Edomites, an ancient people called the Horites dwelt in Mount Seir. The Edomites (living by the sword, Genesis 27:40) overtook and destroyed the Horites and lived on Mount Seir in their place (Deuteronomy 2:12, 22). "Interestingly, the Hebrew word for Seir (*se-ir*) is similar to the word 'hairy' (*se-ar*), the meaning of 'Esau (*esaw*).' Seir, 'Mount Seir,' became synonyms for Edom."[11] The Edomite territory was divided into three areas. The first was the northern section consisting of Bozrah and Punon and was a rough rectangular area about 15 miles wide and 70 miles long which formed the boundary with Moab.[12] This area was at an elevation of 5,000 to 5,700 feet above sea level. The high elevation made it almost impervious to attack. This quadrangle formed a fortified area in Edom, dotted with a series of strongholds. The capital of Edom lay to the west of the "King's Highway" on a massive plateau that towered 1,000 feet above the city of Petra.

The second district of Edom comprised the region south of the Hismeh Valley which was known for its iron and copper mines, a very important source of wealth for the Edomites. In addition to the iron and copper, the important trade routes connecting Mesopotamia and Egypt passed right through the southern extremity of the region, which also contributed greatly to Edom's wealth.[13] The third area of Edom was inhabited mainly by nomadic tribes and was never fully under Edomite control.[14] In 300 B.C. Edom was overthrown by the Nabatæan Arabs, who made the "red rock" hewn city of Petra their capital. Some of the Edomites moved to Idumæa, while others were absorbed by the Nabatæans.[15] When the Romans took over Palestine, the Edomites naturally fell under their jurisdiction. In 120 B.C. John Hyrcanus occupied all of Idumæa and compelled its people to adopt Judaism.[16] From those circumstances in Idumæa came Antipater, the father of Herod (Antipas) the Great. After the fall of Jerusalem in 70 A.D., the Idumæans faded from history, thus ending the Edomites' history.

The First Oracle
Pride and Perdition

The outline of Obadiah's prophecy renders three major oracles, each having its own subdivisions. The first oracle is *Pride and Perdition*. Focusing on verses 2-4 in chapter 1, the passage reads:

> Behold, I have made thee small among the heathen: thou art greatly despised. The pride of thine heart hath deceived thee, thou that dwellest in the clefts of the rock, whose habitation *is* high; that saith in his heart, Who shall bring me down to the ground? Though thou exalt *thyself* as the eagle, and though thou set thy nest among the stars, thence will I bring thee down, saith the Lord. KJV

A salient point that cannot be overlooked: the demise of Edom was not the mere result of the surrounding nations' jealousy and envy. If it were men only with which to be concerned, then Edom's destruction would be avoidable and not inevitable. Though foreign armies did overthrow the Edomites, make no mistake about it, it was by the hand of a sovereign God. In these two verses, the Lord states, "I have made thee *small* among the heathen." (KJV) *The New Living Translation* puts it this way: "I will cut you down to size among the nations."

Throughout history, even unto this very day, great kingdoms have always had to keep a close watch on neighboring nations. Whether they are friend or foe, dominant nations must always be vigilant even amongst allies. Some nations are friendly out of respect, while other nations pretend to be friendly due to strategic, military, or economic superiority. Nations that fear or respect other nations do not rise up against them but seek to keep peaceful relations intact. However, this only remains true until there is a change in perception—a change in heart.

Proverbs 16:7 says, "When a man's ways please the Lord, He makes even his enemies to be at peace with him." What this verse means is, God can make a person whose nature it is to hate you, be at peace with you. It doesn't make a difference who the opposing force is. As in Daniel's case, God caused ferocious lions, which would have normally ripped him to shreds, to be at peace with him. Or, it could be a sworn foe—God can make even the worst enemies peacefully coexist with you and even help you.

This proverb, however, is conditional. It explicitly states, "when a man's ways *please* the Lord…." The question is, what if a man's (or a civilization's) ways *do not* please the Lord? Then God can cause the enemy's fear, respect, and their peace to go away. God can have them see you completely differently. When that happens, you no longer have the same circumstances between you, because they now see you as inferior. They no longer see you as a giant, but in their eyes, God has "cut you down to size," and now they see you as "being small," a nation they can overtake. This is what happened to the Edomites.

At the zenith of their glory, God was setting them up for a fall by making them "small among the nations." Not small geographically or in population, but small in the way of significance, small because of their degradation from a position of respect to one of disrespect. Small because their value was less, small because of their moral decline, small because of their lack of thankfulness and dependence upon God. The Edomites, a great giant, had now become small. Not in stature or size, but in the eyes of God and the eyes of their enemies.

You are Greatly Despised

The next pronouncement was, "thou are greatly despised." The first cousin of disrespect is being the despised. One thing about being on top is that others can't wait to see you fall, or have the pleasure of knocking you down. The Edomites lived on a strategically located rocky plateau. From ancient times, it was referred as Mountain Seir. Their cities were carved out of the solid "red" sandstone. It was stable, secure, and impregnable because it was strategically located at a high elevation.

A high elevation gives you great optics to see what is coming before it gets there, and makes it difficult to reach you if an enemy approaches. It is always better to be situated on the high ground. So the neighboring nations despised the Edomites because they always had to "come up" to them. You had to "come up" to their standards. Being despised is typical whenever the advantages are in someone's else's favor. Whenever a nation has strategic, economic, military, industrial, and standard of living advantages, others will despise you. If not openly, certainly secretly, behind closed doors. But here, they are greatly despised, beyond the norms of typical jealousy and envy to a level of hatred, all because it was part of God's plan to bring the Edomites down.

The Pride of Your Heart Has Deceived You

The next pronouncement was "the pride of your heart has deceived you." The first reality to acknowledge is that nations are only who they are because God made them that way. Nebuchadnezzar found this out from personal experience after being humbled by God for seven years. His words, "All the peoples of the earth are regarded as nothing. He does as he pleases with the powers of heaven and the peoples of the earth," stand for a memorial for all of the nations and rulers that are lifted up in pride. Pride is a potent force of self-destruction. Pride makes you think more of yourself—more than who you really are. Pride makes you think that you are self-sufficient. Self-sufficiency makes you think that you do not need God when in fact without Him you could do nothing.

In Acts 17, we find that it is God who makes the determinations concerning the nations,

> From one man he made all the nations, that they should inhabit the whole earth; and he marked out their appointed times in history and the boundaries of their lands. God did this so that they would seek him and perhaps reach out for him and find him, though he is not far from any one of us. 'For in him we live and move and have our being....
>
> Verses 26-28, NIV

There may be civilizations that feel they may not need God, but in fact, they do. God is the one who determines who, what, when and where a society or nation rises to significance or falls into obscurity. The Bible also states that "The king's heart is like streams of water. Both are under the Lord's control. He turns them in any direction he chooses" (Proverbs 21:1, GW). Though man has freedom of choice, ultimately it is God who gets His way. Therefore, if a nation has power, military strength, natural resources, influence and respect among the nations, it is only because God has permitted it to be so. However, pride negates this understanding. Pride negates giving

God the glory. Pride negates being thankful. Pride breeds nothing but a wicked and arrogant spirit that completely squelches acknowledging God. In Romans 1, this was part of Paul's indictment to the nations when speaking of how and why God's wrath was revealed from heaven against all the ungodliness of the nations (more on this later). The Tyndale Commentary makes the following observation:

> The Bible has much to say about pride, but one simple verse in Proverbs succinctly sums it up, "Pride goes before destruction, And a haughty spirit before a fall" (Proverbs 16:18, NKJV). Pride precedes destruction because "it opposes the first principle of wisdom (the fear of the Lord) and the two great commandments. The proud man is therefore at odds with himself (Proverbs 8:36), his neighbor (Proverbs 13:10) and the Lord (Proverbs 16:5). Therefore, destruction may appropriately come from any quarter."[17]

In Obadiah, the phrase "mount of Esau" is found four times and itself is indicative of power and authority. It is interesting that men put their names upon the very mountains that they did not raise, lands that they did not spread forth, and claim natural resources in which they are not the source. "The earth is the Lord's and the fullness thereof." However, as so many nations throughout history have proclaimed, "this is mine." The Edomites were no different. The very mountains, plateaus, and resources that made them great were not theirs, but belonged to the Lord. It is by His good pleasure that He gives any people anything. However, it is when pride enters that people look at their surroundings and say something similar to what king Nebuchadnezzar said when he boasted, "Is not this the great Babylon I have built as the royal residence, by my mighty power and for the glory of my majesty?" (Daniel 4:30 NIV, 2011). Boy, what a mistake!

It is interesting to note that king Nebuchadnezzar is a Gentile, a non-believer, and not a part of the covenantal promises or blessing of Israel. The Babylonians were not under the Law of Moses. However, none of that makes a difference, because God is the God of the whole earth. Everybody and everything is under His providential control. Whether Jew or Gentile, whether the nations believe in or serve God or not, God is still God.

Dwelling in the Clefts of the Rock

The Edomites were victims of their own pride, self-interest, and wealth. There was no doubt that Edom had some great advantages that summed up in the statement "dwelling in the clefts of the rock." "The root of the arrogance is given by describing the Edomite 'dwelling' as the *clefts of the rocks*, accentuating the rocky impenetrability as well as the height of the Edomite plateau. This served as a natural barrier and stronghold."[18] When a nation has a strategic advantage over its enemies, that nation is in the driver's seat when it comes to matters of foreign affairs, economics, and influence. These advantages contribute to a sense of power and pride. When a nation knows its enemies can't get to them easily to attempt an attack, that bolsters its concept of being secure.

During World War II, the nations bordering Germany had no strategic advantages to stop a German blitz and were simply overrun. However, the Edomites "dwelling in the clefts of the rock" felt as though they were impregnable, relying on the natural defenses and advantages of living "high up." However, this "high living" was not only in reference to the fact of literally living at a high elevation, "in the clefts of the rock," but was also a metaphorical reference to the "standard of living" stemming from the natural resources the Edomites enjoyed in their mountainous territory. As stated earlier, Edom had plenteous iron and copper mines that were some of the richest deposits in the Near East. From these metals, tools and weapons could be made, which relative to the times meant that the Edomites were an advanced, industrialized, and militarized society. In comparison, having rich iron and copper mines would be equivalent to owning most of today's oil reserves. Another strategic advantage was that the trade routes between Mesopotamia and Egypt, extremely important areas for culture, trade, and commerce, passed through Edomite territory. Since Edom was situated in mountainous regions, there were fertile valleys that the Edomites enhanced through irrigation. This agricultural sustenance contributed to their independence and security.

Another factor contributing to Edom's high standard of living was her wealth, which is alluded to in verse 6, "Every nook and cranny of Edom will be searched and looted. Every treasure will be found and taken." (NLT) Her confidence in strong foreign relations is alluded to in verse 7, "All your allies...Your trusted friends...." (NLT) Her confidence in her wisdom (her science and technology, educational institutions, her brilliant economic and business leaders, and innovators and inventors) is alluded to in verse 8, "At that time not a single wise person will be left in the whole land of Edom...," I will destroy everyone who has understanding." And lastly, her military power, alluded to in verse 9, "The mightiest warriors of Teman," is in reference to Edom's elite soldiers. Teman is an ancient reference to Edom.[19]

Who Shall Bring Me Down?

All of the great empires of the earth, at one time or another, have uttered these arrogant words: "Who shall bring me down?" That is, who has the power to change our standard of living? Who has the economic or military power to defeat us? Who dares to try to overthrow us? Who dares to defy us? Who dares to resist our propaganda, our influence, our philosophy, our way of life? Who shall ever bring us down to the ground? We have resources, wealth, influence, allies, military prowess. We control the trade routes and we are elevated higher than the rest! This is the mindset of the arrogant nations who trust in natural power. However, King David makes this observation:

> The Lord foils the plans of the nations; he thwarts the purposes of the peoples. But the plans of the Lord stand

> firm forever, the purposes of his heart through all generations…from his dwelling place he watches all who live on earth—he who forms the hearts of all, who considers everything they do. No king is saved by the size of his army; no warrior escapes by his great strength. A horse is a vain hope for deliverance; despite all its great strength it cannot save.
>
> Psalm 33:10, 14-17, NIV

In this passage, David considers the folly of the nations who suppose that they are actually sovereign. Therefore, foolishly, they trust in their resources, governmental and military power. How foolish are nations that believe that they control their own destiny and do not need God.

Poetically, Obadiah emphasizes the pride of Edom when he says in verse 4, "Though thou exalt *thyself* as the eagle, and though thou set thy nest among the stars, thence will I bring thee down, saith the LORD." Yes, Edom had soared like a mighty eagle unto the very heights of the stars themselves, where they made a nest and dwelt comfortably away from the threat of invasion or attack. In their hearts they said who shall reach to these heights to bring us down? How foolish and arrogant was the disposition of their heart. Therefore, the answer to the question who shall bring me down to the ground, who has the power and might to extinguish the light of Edomite glory—God!

The Second Oracle

The Plunder of Wealth and Prestige

In Obadiah1:5-7 NLT, we find this account,

> "If thieves came at night and robbed you (what a disaster awaits you!), they would not take everything. Those who harvest grapes always leave a few for the poor. But your enemies will wipe you out completely! Every nook and cranny of Edom will be searched and looted. Every treasure will be found and taken. All your allies will turn against you. They will help to chase you from your land. They will promise you peace while plotting to deceive and destroy you. Your trusted friends will set traps for you, and you won't even know about it."

Emphasizing the total plunder of Edom from invaders, the prophet sympathizes rhetorically by emphasizing the antithesis, when he asks, "even if thieves came to steal from you, would they not leave something behind? On the other hand, if harvesters come to harvest crops do they not leave some produce behind for the poor to glean?" The answer is, these invaders will not. They will have no mercy or any consideration. The plundering will be total. Who will these plundering agents be? The Edomite allies, whom the Edomites trusted. There is a very thin line between ally and enemy. One bad move can change a good relationship between nations into a bad one (see 2 Samuel 10), especially when it comes by God's sovereign judgment. All of the Edomites' wealth and prestige will be sucked up by the treachery of their jealous and despising allies. Walvoord and Zuck note, "ironically, Edom deceived by her own pride would then be deceived by her allies! What an alarming strategy—not an attack by a known enemy, but an ambush by an ally."[20]

The Third Oracle

Destruction

In Obadiah1:8-9, we find these predictions,

> "In that day," declares the Lord, "will I not destroy the wise men of Edom, those of understanding in the mountains of Esau? Your warriors, Teman, will be terrified, and everyone in Esau's mountains will be cut down in the slaughter. NIV

Here, we find the account of the destruction of the "wise men" of Edom. As far back as in Job's day, the Edomites were known for their wise men (see Job 2:11, Jeremiah 49:7). Nations prosper when there is wise counsel within leadership and when leaders have access to a host of wise counsel (Proverbs 11:14). However, the destruction of a society's wise men, literature, libraries, the institutions of higher learning, along with the infrastructure of the same, were common casualties during ancient times. To this very day, we can only postulate as to how the Egyptians built the pyramids because when Alexander the Great conquered Egypt, the Egyptian libraries were destroyed. Secondly, Edom's military capability was also destroyed. No civilization can maintain itself without having military defenses. The fact that the elite soldiers were destroyed meant that Edom had zero chances to regain a foothold as a thriving nation again. All three of the essential elements of a thriving nation were predicted to be destroyed in Obadiah's prophecy. And as history bears out, the Edomites are no more.

This brief grammatical-historical perspective shows that the prophecy by Obadiah regarding the Edomites does find itself in historic fulfillment. And it is my opinion that Obadiah's message, at least in his mind, was in reference to the nation he knew as the Edomites of antiquity. It is not the author's intention to suggest that Obadiah had any other future nation in mind.

However, considering the aforementioned Obadiah in the midst of his prophecy to the Edomites, God did have other nation(s) in mind thousands of years later when in the following verses He, through Obadiah, writes: "The day of the Lord is near for all nations. As you have done, it will be done to you; your deeds will return upon your own head" (Obadiah 1:15, NIV). Clearly, Obadiah could not have understood the significance of the eschatological ramifications of this passage. Nor could he have possibly understood the vast time element as to the scope of the latter fulfillment of this prophecy. It is evident that this prophecy is given from the Lord's perspective, because the prophecy states the day of the Lord is "near." Obviously, it is not near from a human perspective, but to Him who is eternal, where one day is as a thousand years and a thousand years as a day (see 2 Peter 3:8), it was just days away. Therefore, the Edomites of antiquity serve as a template to why God will judge the concerned nations in the future.

In chapter one, we covered an important law in interpreting prophecy called "the law of double reference." We defined the Law of Double Reference as:

> A prophecy may focus upon two different events separated by a vast amount of time as to their fulfillment, but contained in one prophecy. Often God gave a message for the prophet's day, as well as had a prophecy for a future time.

As it pertains to this aspect of Obadiah's prophecy, clearly there is an unambiguous double reference by introducing eschatological terminology called *the day of the Lord*, verse 15. The "day of the Lord" was a common theme throughout the Old Testament and the New Testament and is found in Isaiah 2:12, 13:6,9; Ezekiel 13:5, 30:3; Joel 1:15, 2:1, 11, 31; 3:14; Amos 5:18,20; Obadiah 15, Zephaniah 1:7, 14; Zechariah 14:1; Malachi 4:5; Acts 2:20; 1 Thessalonians 5:2; 2 Thessalonians 2:2; and 2 Peter 3:10. It is characterized as a day of: *anger, battle, bitterness, darkness, destruction, dread*, and a day of *wrath*. It is a prophetic period during the final days of this present age that culminates with the return of the Lord in glory, to rule on earth during a period known as the Millennium. Therefore, the day of the Lord is yet in the future, which gives a futuristic view to Obadiah's ancient prophecy concerning the Edomites. The question is who represents the modern-day Edomites?

The Spiritualization of Names and Terms

As a footnote to this study, it is important to understand the incidence where names in the Bible were spiritualized, meaning that another name was given to a person or a place based upon the attributes and characterization as God saw it, not according to the actual name. For example, in Revelation Babylon, whose name means *confusion*,[21] is also characterized as the "*great whore*" (Revelation 17:1; 19:2) because she has committed "*fornication*" (Revelation 18:3; 19:2). Here the characterization "great whore" is in reference to Babylon's lewd wickedness that has seduced (like a promiscuous and unfaithful prostitute) the kings and nations of the earth through her alluring wealth and beauty, while hiding her true abominable, diseased, and infectious nature. From God's perspective, who judges the heart of matters, Babylon is called by its spiritual nature, a great whore who commits fornication.

Naming a location after its spiritual attributes can also be seen in Revelation 11, where Jerusalem is called *Sodom and Egypt* (Revelation 11:8). Ironically, the average Jewish person would be repulsed at the idea of being characterized as these nations that represent uncleanness, lasciviousness, and bondage. However, that's the very way God saw Jerusalem, the city that Jesus lamented over who killed God's prophets (see Luke 13:34).

Another example of the spiritual symbolical use of names is also found in Revelation 2:20, where God calls a prophetess there *Jezebel.* Here is a part of the Lord's rebuke: "Nevertheless, I have this against you: You tolerate that woman Jezebel, who calls herself a prophet. By her teaching she misleads my servants into sexual immorality and the eating of food sacrificed to idols." (NIV) John MacArthur gives us this insight,

> Jezebel undoubtedly was not the false prophetess's real name, but like the infamous wife of King Ahab, she was Satan's agent to corrupt God's people. Therefore the Lord branded her with the symbolic name Jezebel. The Old Testament Jezebel was an unspeakably vile woman—so much so that the Bible names marrying her as the most evil thing wicked King Ahab did.[22]

Again, we have God's characterization of the "prophetess," of whom the congregants of the church of Thyatira obviously had a more accepting opinion (Revelations 2:18-25). This underscores the fact that how a people or a nation sees themselves can be diametrically opposed to how God sees them. Nineveh, a great, powerful, influential, and large city, saw themselves as being the pinnacle of culture, achievement, and success, but God, who was about to destroy that city, saw them as "a hundred and twenty thousand people who cannot tell their right hand from their left..."(Jonah 4:11, NIV). God actually had mercy on Nineveh, a population of spiritual idiots, by sending Jonah there to warn them of the impending divine judgment and destruction. However, Jonah's message calling the Ninevites to repent was heeded, and judgment did not come on that generation but was delayed (more on this later).

CHAPTER 3
THE UNITED STATES
ISRAEL'S BIG BROTHER

No one can doubt that the United States and Israel have a special and long-standing relationship. Israel is America's closest ally in the Middle East, and America is Israel's closest ally amongst the host of nations around the world. The ongoing bond between America and Israel stands upon the foundation of shared values and common interests. During the more than six decades of Israel's existence as a nation, the Israelis have looked to the United States for political backing, financial and military assistance and defense, and diplomatic support. America, in turn, has viewed Israel with a special appreciation for its successful effort to follow the Western democratic tradition, its remarkable and rapid economic development, and its constant struggle against neighboring, unrelentingly hostile nations. When asked by Soviet Premier Aleksei Kosygin why the U.S. supported Israel when there were 80 million Arabs and only three million Israelis, President Lyndon Johnson summed it up in four words, "Because it is right."

America's support for the establishment of Israel as a sovereign nation goes back to the late 1800s and early 1900s. Most notably, America backed the *Balfour Declaration* introduced to Parliament by Arthur Balfour, former Prime Minster of the United Kingdom and Foreign Secretary at the time. The Balfour Declaration proposed that the British Government facilitate the establishment of an Israeli state in Palestine. President Woodrow Wilson was a supporter of this movement and stated: "The allied nations with the fullest concurrence of our government and people are agreed that in Palestine shall be laid the foundations of a Jewish Commonwealth."[23]

Several American administrations also gave their assent and support to the establishment of Israel. After leaving office, President Warren Harding expressed his administration's support of this noble enterprise. President Harding stated, "It is impossible for one who has studied at all the services of the Hebrew people to avoid the faith that they will one day be restored to their historic national home and there enter on a new and yet greater phase of their contribution to the advance of humanity."[24]

Calvin Coolidge expressed his "sympathy with the deep and intense longing which finds such fine expression in the Jewish National Homeland in Palestine."[25] "Palestine which was desolate for centuries, is now renewing its youth and vitality through enthusiasm, hard work, and self-sacrifice of the Jewish pioneers who toil there in a spirit of peace and social justice," observed Herbert Hoover.[26]

Congress was no less sympathetic to the Zionist objective, as evidenced when the joint Congressional resolutions of 1922 and 1944 unanimously passed an endorsement of the Balfour Declaration.[27]

Clearly, Israel's founding (May 14, 1948) was preceded by decades of efforts to establish a national homeland for the Jewish people. The 1917 Balfour Declaration asserted the British Government's support for the creation "in Palestine of a national home for the Jewish people." Following the end of World War I (1914-1918), the League of Nations entrusted Great Britain with the *Mandate for Palestine*. Immediately after the end of British mandate on May 14, 1948, the State of Israel was proclaimed, and the United States was the first nation to grant de facto recognition to the new Jewish State—11 minutes after the proclamation.[28] "I had faith in Israel before it was established, I have faith in it now," President Harry Truman said on May 26, 1952. "I believe it has a glorious future before it—not just another sovereign nation, but as an embodiment of the great ideals of our civilization."[29]

Ever since its establishment, America has had a very close relationship with Israel. John F. Kennedy stated: "This nation, from the time of President Woodrow Wilson, has established and continued a tradition of friendship with Israel because we are committed to all free societies that seek a path to peace and honor individual rights. In the prophetic spirit of Zionism all free men today look to a better world and in the experience of Zionism we know that it takes courage and perseverance and dedication to achieve it."

Said Lyndon Johnson, "The United States and Israel share many common objectives...chief of which is the building of a better world in which every nation can develop its resources and develop them in freedom and peace." The inspiration behind Johnson's feelings, like those of many other Americans, came from the Bible. "Most if not all of you have very deep ties with the land and with the people of Israel, as I do, for my Christian faith sprang from your…the Bible stories are woven into my childhood memories as the gallant struggle of modern Jews to be free of persecution is also woven into our souls."[30]

President Richard Nixon asserted that the United States stands by its friends and that "Israel is one of its friends." His successor, Gerald Ford, reaffirmed his "commitment to the security and future of Israel is based upon basic morality as well as enlightened self-interest. Our role in supporting Israel honors our own heritage."[31]

Jimmy Carter once said, "The United States has a warm and a unique relationship of friendship with Israel that is morally right. It is compatible with our deepest religious convictions, and it is right in terms of America's own strategic interests. We are committed to Israel's security, prosperity, and future as a land that has so much to offer the world."[32]

Unlike his predecessors, Ronald Reagan was the first President to state explicitly that Israel was a strategic asset to the United States. Reagan stated, "Only by full appreciation of the critical role the State of Israel plays in our strategic calculus can we build the foundation for thwarting Moscow's designs on territories and resources vital to our security and our national well-being."[33]

George H.W. Bush said: "The friendship, the alliance between the United States and Israel is strong and solid, built upon a foundation of shared democratic values, of shared history and heritage, that sustains the life of our two countries. The emotional bond of our people transcends politics. Our strategic cooperation—and I renew today our determination that go forward—is a source of mutual security. And the United States' commitment to the security of Israel remains unshakeable. We may differ over some policies from time to time, individual policies, but never over the principle."[34]

Bill Clinton made this powerful and inspirational statement, "Our relationship would never vary from its allegiance to the shared values, the shared religious heritage, the shared democratic politics which have made the relationship between the United States and Israel a special—even on occasion a wonderful—relationship."[35]

George W. Bush echoed the sentiments of nearly every President that came before him. "We will speak up for our principles and we will stand up for our friends in the world," Bush said. "And one of our most important friends in the world is the State of Israel."[36]

Though under his administration U.S. and Israeli relations have been tested and stretched due to many foreign policy differences, chiefly over the Iran nuclear arms deal, President Barack Obama stated that "we [America] stand with Israel as a Jewish democratic state because we know that Israel is born of firmly held values that we, as Americans, share: a culture committed to justice, a land that welcomes the weary, a people devoted to *tikkun olam* (healing the world)." Furthermore, "We're going to keep standing with our Israeli friends and allies."

According to the U.S. Department of State, the U.S. provides over $3 billion in foreign military financing annually. The U.S. also participates in high-level exchanges with Israel which include joint military exercises, military research, and weapons research and development, including enhanced cooperation in counterterrorism. The United States is still Israel's number one trading partner. The top five U.S. exports to Israel are: diamonds, machinery, agricultural products, aircraft, and optic and medical instruments. The top five U.S. imports from Israel are: diamonds, pharmaceutical products, machinery, optic and medical instruments, and agricultural products.[38]

All of the aforementioned is to emphasize the point that since the beginning, America—like a big brother—has been there to support Israel, and even to defend Israel. Their interest and ours is intertwined, sharing many things in common, including the Abrahamic covenantal blessing where the Bible declares,

I will make you into a great nation, and I will bless you;

> I will make your name great, and you will be a blessing. I will bless those who bless you, and whoever curses you I will curse; and all peoples on earth will be blessed through you.
>
> Genesis 12:2-3, NIV

According to God's Abrahamic promises to Israel, all the nations that bless Israel will be blessed by God. Conversely, all the nations that curse Israel will be cursed by God. Right now, the U.S. and Israel enjoy a good relationship, even though it has been strained under the Obama administration. This is and has been certainly favorable for America, which in many ways is blessed. However, this also places America in another "Esau"-like role because America "is like" a big brother to Israel, just as Esau was the older brother to Jacob, whose name God later changed to Israel (see Genesis 32:28).

Though some may balk at this suggested comparison, the fact is that America's relationship with Israel, though good at the moment, is just one piece of the puzzle that places this great nation in the crosshairs of prophecy, destiny, and eventual devastation and demise.

In our thematic text, we find seven aspects of Obadiah's prophecy that align directly to the United States of America. They are:

- I have made thee small among the nations.
- Thou art greatly despised.
- The pride of your heart has deceived you.
- Dwelling in the clefts of the Rock.
- Exalt thyself as the eagle.

- A nest among the stars.
- As you have done, it shall be done to you.

Chapter 4
America In Decline
"I Have Made Thee Small Among the Nations"

Thus far, in this study we have examined the ancient civilization called the Edomites. We have examined them from a biblical history tracing all the way back to Esau, their progenitor. We have examined the Edomites culturally and nationally, including their rise from obscurity to prominence. We have examined them spiritually, concerning the origins of their relationship and disposition toward God, which revealed a disdain for the things pertaining to Him. We have examined how the actions of Esau, when he sold his birthright for a bowl of red soup, impacted his whole bloodline, thus sealing the Edomites' doom as a culture and a nation. We also covered how there is a transition in Obadiah's prophecy that moves the focus from the historic to the futuristic. Concerning this transition, we covered how the hermeneutical concept called the "law of double reference" applies to this prophecy.

Going forward, we will examine aspects of Obadiah's prophecy that correlates directly to the United States of

America. There will be those who disagree with the conclusions made in this book—that is to be expected. As has been the case with many nations, few have ever taken seriously a prophecy concerning their demise—yet they fell. This was a great dilemma to prophets like Habakkuk and Jeremiah, who were vehemently opposed because their message to the people was one of judgment and captivity. Therefore, I expect no different from some of those who read this book that see nothing wrong with America. However, I do pray that there will be many who will see the light and gain an understanding of things to come concerning America—a once-great nation that is up to its neck in debauchery and running headlong toward destruction.

As I stated, there are seven amazing prophecies found in verses 2 through 4 of Obadiah that correlate to the United States of America: "I have made thee small among the nations," "Thou art greatly despised," "The pride of your heart has deceived you," "Dwelling in the clefts of the Rock," "Exalt thyself as the eagle," "A nest among the stars," and "As you have done to others, it shall be done to you."

To understand this first prophecy, we must build upon some important biblical precepts, the first being that it is God that makes a nation great. In Romans, the apostle Paul makes his case for God's sovereign control exercised through His divine election when he asserts, "For Scripture says to Pharaoh: 'I raised you up for this very purpose, that I might display my power in you and that my name might be proclaimed in all the earth'" (Romans 9:17, NIV). Here, Paul is quoting from Exodus 9:16 to emphasize his point that Pharaoh was the ruler of a mighty nation by God's doing according to the divine plan that He had for Israel, Egypt historically, and as an object lesson for everyone else who reads this account. What is noteworthy here is that the Egyptians were Gentiles and pagan idol worshippers, not believers, yet God was still sovereign over their affairs. The notion that God is involved only with "believing people and nations" is false. God is God over all the heaven and the earth. Not believing in or acknowledging God does not undo or negate His divine sovereignty.

Considering this, if it is God that makes a nation great, as we know of the Egyptians, Babylonians, and many others, it is also God that brings a nation down. God has many ways to bring down kingdoms. A few are: He can rain down fire and brimstone, He can send an angel to wipe them out, He can let them implode from internal wickedness, He can cause famines or floods, or He can cause their enemies to overtake them. Whatever God decides to do, He is sovereign, and no one can say to him, "What are you doing?" (see Daniel 4:35).

As with the ancient Edomites, God said, "I have made you small among the nations." As we covered in a previous chapter, "I will make you small" carries some important inferences. First, God is saying I will *make you* small, or I will cause you to become small. The tacit implication here is that something large, as the *New Living Translation* would say, is being "cut down to size." What this suggests is not being reduced in population or territory but in significance and influence.

Yes, America has the most powerful and advanced military on earth, but with all of our technology, armament, and troops, America did not win in the Korean Conflict but settled for an armistice (ceasefire agreement). We could not defeat the ragtag army of North Vietnam and had to pull out. We are having difficulty winning in Afghanistan, and we couldn't bring democracy to Iraq even though we claimed victory there and had tens of thousands of troops there. We could not back down the Assad regime in Syria, after drawing a red line in the sand about the use of chemical weapons. We could not stop assaults on our embassies such as Benghazi, Libya, Cairo, Egypt, and others. We have difficulty stopping ISIS (the Islamic State of Iraq and Syria), who has clearly defied American interests and beheaded our citizens in public. After America withdrew from Iraq, this left a power void that ISIS assumed. In a movement that is sweeping through Iraq and Syria, ISIS has momentum that American bombing, cruise missiles, and drones alone cannot stop. These are just a few examples of how America's glory is fading on the international stage due to the loss of respect, status, and significance.

On September 11, 2001, America was brought to its knees when members of al-Qaeda hijacked American passenger jets and crashed them into the World Trade Center towers and the Pentagon. Americans were dumbfounded, as this was the worst attack by a foreign entity on the mainland of the United States. No one had ever pulled off such an astoundingly bold attack before. Not since Pearl Harbor had America been rocked by an attack of this magnitude. In the wake of this horrific terrorist attack, our nation has never been the same. Now we know we are attackable. Now we know that we are not impenetrable. Now we know that death and carnage can be brought to our shores by a foreign entity. The unnerving aspect about that is that it wasn't done by a foreign military but by a sophisticated terrorist group. Though many changes have occurred in Homeland Security, our government cannot guarantee the citizens of the United States that an attack like this or worse will not happen again. As a matter of fact, many predict that it will happen again.

What has contributed to all of the upheaval? The answer is, the world and our enemies no longer see America as a great nation to be feared and respected. But they see Americans as fat, spoiled, wasteful, and wealthy, acting as if they own the world and that the world revolves around America. They see us as arrogant but stupid. They see us as a society given over to debauchery, hedonism, and excess. Ironically, we as Americans see ourselves as "the stuff," while many others around the world see us as weakened and wicked.

Due to this sense of entitlement that Americans have, countries that we once considered as Third World are now beating us in areas such as technology and manufacturing. For example, America, though it has some of the best schools in the world, lags far behind other nations in educational achievement. Here are some astounding statistics from the NPR (National Public Radio) website.

> American 15-year-olds continue to turn in flat results in a test that measures students' proficiency in reading, math and science worldwide, failing to crack the global top 20. The Program for International Student Assessment, or PISA, collects test results from 65 countries for its rankings, which come out every three years. The latest results, from 2012, show that U.S. students ranked below average in math among the world's most-developed countries. They were close to average in science and reading.
>
> "In mathematics, 29 nations and other jurisdictions outperformed the United States by a statistically significant margin, up from 23 three years ago," reports Education Week. "In science, 22 education systems scored above the U.S. average, up from 18 in 2009."[39]

This is why so many of our technology companies struggle with filling technology jobs, because Americans are not competitive with other nations around the world that outperform our students. Therefore, many of our own companies outsource and manufacture overseas. Many immigrants to our country know that they have a leg up educationally, but lack the opportunity in their countries. If given half the chance, they come to America to prosper, all the while despising Americans who think they are entitled and have things handed to them.

All of this is indicative of how others around the world see us. However, what is really behind how nations perceive one another is God. God can cause your enemies to be at peace with you. He can make them flee when no one is chasing them. He can turn their heart against you, and He can cause them to rise up against you.

Economic Decline

Economically, America no longer has the status that it used to have. In April 2011, America's credit rating was downgraded from AAA to AA for the first time in history, causing some serious international embarrassment and concern. Part of the reason for this downgrade was due to all of America's unbridled spending leading to trillions of dollars of debt. Ironically, our dollar is still very strong and stable among world currencies, even though the dollar has not had any backing in decades since Nixon took it off the gold standard. Though this may come as a surprise to some, other than the government's word, the fact is that the U.S. dollar isn't backed by anything.

The dollar is controlled by a private banking cartel misleadingly called the "Federal Reserve Bank," which is a private bank, "not Federal and has no part of the government." The Federal Reserve Bank determines how much value our dollar has and how much to put into circulation. America is one of the top 20 largest debtor nations in the world, owing billions of dollars to nations like China. Currently, the United States government's debt is over 18 trillion dollars. To understand how much money that is, if you spent $10,000,000 a day, it would take you over

4,931 years to spend 18 trillion dollars. Most Americans will never have $100,000 in the bank at one time in their entire life, let alone $1,000,000.

The Great Recession of 2008 was the worst economic downturn in this country since the Great Depression. The recession was triggered by billions of dollars of bad mortgage debt that started a chain reaction where major corporations, banks, and financial institutions all went belly up. Senator Rand Paul stated that "in the last few years we have created 4 trillion dollars of money out of thin air. While since 2006 we have doubled our national debt." Senator Paul went on to say, "Prosperity cannot be created out of thin air by a central bank (the Federal Reserve Bank). Because of all of our debt and an unrestrained federal reserve bank, bankers and financial institutions around the world will start losing confidence in the American dollar. You cannot restore confidence in the American dollar by printing more paper money." He also said, "Our prosperity is due to our liberty, but now our liberty is being threatened, so then will our prosperity." Right now, the American dollar is still the primary reserve currency in the world, but when, not if, that changes, America will face unparalleled economic upheaval. America's massive debt is being held up by thin paper dollars. Ironically, on those dollars, the national motto is written, "In God We Trust," a God that clearly America has turned her back on. The middle class in America is being squeezed out of existence, while there is a growing underclass that has little hope of achieving that illusive "American dream."

America has been turned into a nation of consumers who are controlled by the interests of huge corporate conglomerates that are purely profit-driven. The corporations don't care about our health and well-being. All they care about is ways to transfer your money to their coffers while making you feel good about it. The greatest transfer of wealth happens when millions of relatively poor individuals take their hard-earned dollars and transfer it to the huge corporations that tell you what products to purchase. In the film *The Devil Wears Prada*, Meryl Streep's character Miranda Priestly chides Anne Hathaway's character Andrea (Andy) Sachs when she says:

> "You think this has nothing to do with you. You go to your closet and you select...I don't know...that lumpy blue sweater, for instance because you're trying to tell the world that you take yourself too seriously to care about what you put on your back....However, that blue (sweater) represents millions of dollars and countless jobs and it's sort of comical how you think that you've made a choice that exempts you from the fashion industry when, in fact, you're wearing the sweater that was selected for you by the people in this room...."[40]

This is one of the many tongue-lashings that Ms. Sachs had to endure in the film, but it is an important one. Though this film is fictional, this statement is based on fact. The clothes consumers buy in stores are what has been chosen for them to wear. People think that they are making a free choice. That's the illusion of product marketing; give people the freedom to buy what has been chosen for them by someone else, appealing to their emotions, thereby making them feel good about themselves. This is mainly the brainchild of Sigmund Freud's American nephew Edward Bernays, father of the term "public relations," who expanded upon his uncle's theories concerning the masses. Bernays, like Freud, believed that the masses are controlled by irrational forces, and that through stimulating our innermost desires with consumer products, the masses' irrational behavior and emotions could be controlled. This philosophy revolutionized marketing psychology, public relations, and product development as we know it today.

In Bernays' philosophy, companies didn't sell products to a person's intellect, they sold them to their emotions. In other words, the main emphasis is not just on needed products, but products that make you "feel better about yourself." Companies wanted you to drive this model of car *and feel great* or smoke this brand of cigarette and *be a man*. They would convince you that if you wear this type of gym shoe, *you will run faster* and *jump higher* or wear this brand of lipstick or perfume and *all the men will want you*. By appealing to our emotions and self-esteem and providing wanted but not needed products, companies could pacify people into becoming passive consumers who would rather be entertained than informed and whose main interests lie in self-centeredness and self-gratification instead of activist citizens, aware of what's really happening.

The primary method of pacification is delivered through our television sets and multimedia devices. Why are there so many televised sports events, game shows, award shows, weekly dramas, and comedies produced? It is to keep the masses controlled and pacified through the media that is controlled by the same corporate interests, many of which produce both the products and the television programs.

These same corporate interests are the ones who decide which programs are aired because they are the ones who buy the airtime to make the programs possible while also promoting the next products to buy. These are the same corporate interests that have the lobbyists in Washington that influence laws and legislation that affect our lives. This is why corporations can make food products that make us sick, cigarettes that cause cancer, medicines that have terrible side-effects, and products that are dangerous—all with the expressed purpose of increasing their bottom line. They make tons of money from products that can last on the store shelves for months, taste good, but have little to no nutritional value, and even promote diseases like cancer and diabetes. Why? It's all for the love of money, which is the root of all evil (1 Timothy 6:10). It is a profit-driven, "greed is good" mentality. We live in a country that will entice a kid to want a pair of $250 gym shoes made in some overseas sweatshop from the labor of some child forced to work for pennies a day under cruel conditions. Ironically, the same kid wearing those gym shoes could be killed over them by another kid who doesn't have the $250 to buy them.

It is this type of capitalism that cares nothing about

the consumers other than keeping them buying something new, whether they need it or not. Look at technology products like smartphones. Lines stretch for blocks to buy the latest phone that people probably don't need. This is the America that has been created by greed. Whereas many Americans are led to believe that America is a "democratic society," this is only partially true. We are more of a capitalist society that is run by the "golden rule" where he who has the "gold" rules. This consumer-based mechanism is fueled by the love of money, hence the economic decline. Economic decline does not mean necessarily that there will be a total collapse of the financial system where all the banks will have no money, but it does mean that a nation which puts "In God We Trust" on their dollars, but has *no trust* in the living God, has by default made money their God. America is in economic decline because it is not investing in its people, but it invests in the art of taking money from the people no matter what the price.

Jesus said, "No one can serve two masters. Either you will hate the one and love the other, or you will be devoted to the one and despise the other. You cannot serve both God and money" (Luke 16:13, NIV). If money is the God that America trusts, then America no longer has a God that can save it. This certainly is a most tragic reason for an economic decline.

Moral Decline

Another reason why America is being made small among the nations is because of her rapid moral decline. Remember, no nation pulls itself up by its own bootstraps; it is God that exalts or debases a nation. In Proverbs 14:34 the Bible teaches, "Righteousness exalts a nation, but sin condemns any people." (NIV) Also in Psalm 9:17, the Bible also gives this solemn warning, "The wicked shall be turned into hell, *and* all the nations that forget God."(KJV) There is no ambiguity concerning either of these passages. Righteousness is what exalts a nation, not its GNP, its military power, or political influence, but only its ability to follow the laws and precepts of God. By living in accordance with the leadership and guidance of God through His divine precepts, a nation will be prosperous and experience good success. When a nation is governed by a system of just laws and wise, prudent leaders who are not given into bribes and the corrupting influences of oligarchs or kleptocracies, then righteousness and equality will be to the benefit of all of its citizens. However, sin brings about wickedness that corrodes and corrupts the very foundation of a nation until it is destroyed.

Attacks against the right to life, prayer being taken out of the schools, the protest against the use of religious symbols, even a switching away from saying "Merry Christmas" during Christmas season are just a few of the indicators of America's moral decline.

On June 26, 2015, the United States was changed forever when the United States Supreme Court ruled in a contentious 5-4 ruling that gay and lesbian couples can marry in all 50 states. Though many saw this as a great victory for civil rights, the fact remains that this is a moral issue that will have a devastating impact on this nation. The legal ramifications have already begun to surface. In Rowan County, Kentucky, County Clerk Kim Davis was jailed for contempt of court for refusing to issue marriage licenses to same-sex couples, despite the Supreme Court's ruling that cleared the way for gay marriage nationwide. Citing her faith in God and the authority of Scripture, Kim stated that to issue these licenses would be a violation of her religious freedom, God's Word, and her conscience. No matter where you fall on whether she should have resigned rather than be jailed is an ongoing debate among believers as to which action was most appropriate. We must certainly understand that Kim Davis will be among countless Christians who will be openly persecuted right here in America. This is heartbreaking, because just a few decades ago, this was a nation with the motto "In God We Trust" and whose Pledge of Allegiance proudly proclaimed that we were "one nation under God," but now this same nation jails individuals who stand up for the principles that honor the same God.

However, the broader question that remains is what causes a nation to get to this point? How has America passed laws that defy the very order concerning the institution of marriage between a man and a woman set in place by God since the beginning? To answer this question, we must turn to the first chapter of Romans.

> The wrath of God is being revealed from heaven against all the godlessness and wickedness of people, who suppress the truth by their wickedness. For although they knew God, they neither glorified him as God nor gave thanks to him, but their thinking became futile and their foolish hearts were darkened. Although they claimed to be wise, they became fools. Therefore God gave them over in the sinful desires of their hearts to sexual impurity for the degrading of their bodies with one another. They exchanged the truth about God for a lie, and worshiped and served created things rather than the Creator—who is forever praised. Amen. Because of this, God gave them over to shameful lusts. Even their women exchanged natural sexual relations for unnatural ones. In the same way the men also abandoned natural relations with women and were inflamed with lust for one another. Men committed shameful acts with other men, and received in themselves the due penalty for their error.
>
> Romans 1:18, 21-22, 24-27, NIV

An entire book can be written on these verses in Romans. Obviously, time will not permit the fullest examination of this text. It should also be noted that the following commentary is not meant to single out homosexuality or the Supreme Court ruling concerning same-sex marriage. It should be noted that the "wrath of God is revealed from heaven against *all ungodliness and wickedness of people who suppress the truth by their wickedness*." However, a society that is given over to homosexuality itself is a moral indicator of where a nation stands with God.

Paul begins his indictment of the nations by identifying the downward spiral and digression that occur when a nation, people, or kingdom rejects God's person, sovereignty, and moral law. In verse 21, Paul states, "For although they knew God, they neither glorified him as God nor gave thanks to him, but their thinking became futile and their foolish hearts were darkened." What this passage identifies is a willful and intentional rejection of God. This leads to a foolish heart and a darkened mind.

God is the Father of lights, the glorious light of life, power, and divine revelation. This is the light that lights every man when he comes into the world (see James 1:17, John 1:4-9), whom the foolish and darkened have by their own vile volition rejected. They do this by willful suppression of the truth. Willfully suppressing the truth leads to rejecting even the very idea of God. This furthers the downward spiral leading to the irreverence of God, and a state of not being thankful towards the sovereignty, goodness, mercy, and grace of God. This then, leads to people *professing themselves to be wise but becoming fools.* Our schools teach the "big bang theory" and "evolution" as an established fact that is clearly a lie, subtly implanting the notion that there is no God. Romans 1:20 states, "For since the creation of the world God's invisible qualities—his eternal power and divine nature—have been clearly seen, being understood from what has been made, so that people are without excuse." The heavens, the earth, and all creation declare the glory of God, and set the basis for natural revelation. Therefore, men are without excuse because it is rationally undeniable. You do not need a Bible to comprehend the obvious.

By the continuous rejection of God, in all facets of human life, educationally, scientifically, governmentally, legally, morally, and practically, at a certain point God simply pulls back and leaves people to their own wicked propensities and vices. People have no idea of the totality of wickedness resident in their hearts. In the *King James Version*, Jeremiah 17:9 puts it this way, "The heart *is* deceitful above all *things*, and desperately wicked: who can know it?" Without God, people are exceedingly sinful and capable of every form of wickedness imaginable. This leads to exchanging "the truth of God for a lie," where things that were once wrong are now right, and where things that are right are now considered wrong (see Isaiah 5:20). Clearly this is evident here in America, where the things that just a few decades ago would have been considered vile and shameful are now celebrated as right, good, and legal.

A society that continuously rejects God, exalting wicked human rights above God and His moral law in a constant thrust towards secularization or freedom from God and religion, ends up being a nation totally given over to wickedness. Of course, this wickedness will be seen as political correctness and righteousness. Through constant suppression of righteousness, the wickedness and debauchery of the unregenerate human heart then oozes openly out into society. One of these forms of expressed wickedness that have oozed out into society is an open embracing and legalization of homosexuality. For any society that constantly rejects God and His righteousness the Bible warns,

> That is why God abandoned them to their shameful desires. Even the women turned against the natural way to have sex and instead indulged in sex with each other. And the men, instead of having normal sexual relations with women, burned with lust for each other. Men did shameful things with other men, and as a result of this sin, they suffered within themselves the penalty they deserved. Since they thought it foolish to acknowledge God, he abandoned them to their foolish thinking and let them do things that should never be done.
>
> Romans 1:26-28, NLT

This new legal wave of wickedness sweeping across America will change this nation forever. Every quarter of our society, at all levels of education, all levels of government, private and public sectors, even churches, Christian denominations, Bible translations, and Christian doctrine shall not go untainted. The children born in this untoward generation will come into the world where this form of wickedness is the norm, therefore by default accepted as righteous. Anyone who dares speak out against homosexuality will suffer persecution from individuals, the courts, and society.

This is why the doctrine or gospel of "inclusion" is false. Yes, God loves all sinners, that is why He sent Jesus to die for the sin of the world, because He so loved the world. Nevertheless, He *is not* endorsing our wickedness and encouraging us to stay in it! In 1 Corinthians, chapter 6, the Bible admonishes,

> Or do you not know that wrongdoers will not inherit the kingdom of God? Do not be deceived: Neither the sexually immoral nor idolaters nor adulterers nor men who have sex with men nor thieves nor the greedy nor drunkards nor slanderers nor swindlers will inherit the kingdom of God. And that is what some of you were. But you were washed, you were sanctified, you were justified in the name of the Lord Jesus Christ and by the Spirit of our God.
>
> Verses 9-11, NIV 2011

Clearly, this passage is not only about same-sex sins, as other sins equally disqualifying for the kingdom of God are delineated as well. The point is that no matter what you were in bondage to you *can* "come out" and be washed and sanctified by the Holy Spirit. Staying in sin guarantees you *will not* enter the kingdom of God, no matter what the church that you attend teaches you. Churches can't save anyone. Only God can do that, and He sets the criteria for salvation according to His Word. People and their philosophies, doctrines, and assurances cannot save you, only God can. Therefore, He admonishes, "Do not be deceived." America in its quest for human rights has rejected God's moral law that is the only law capable of delivering people from the consequences of the wickedness of their own hearts. Isaiah 3:9 warns,

> The look on their faces testifies against them; they parade their sin like Sodom; they do not hide it. Woe to them! They have brought disaster upon themselves.
>
> NIV 2011

Sodom (where we get the English word *sodomy*) was a society wholly given over to *open* homosexuality. God's disapproval of this lifestyle which is contrary to the created order is documented in Genesis 18-19, hundreds of years prior to the giving of the Mosaic Law. Concerning the Isaiah 3:9 passage, the *Tyndale Commentary* states,

> ...guilt is compounded by the fact that it is not regarded by the people as their guilty secret and they have no sense of guilt. Sin is no longer sin, it is the new morality. Thus it is that societies collapse.[41]

This commentary speaks of "a new morality" on which the "new laws" and the "gospel of inclusion" are based. Therefore, this is not an *alarmist* or *homophobic* point of view. This is what "thus sayeth the Lord." God said that societies given over to such wickedness are headed for destruction. It is very important that people understand that these are "God's words," written thousands of years ago, warning any nation of the perils of going down this path.

Interestingly, the *NIV* identifies a particular trait of this movement, that "they *parade* their sin like Sodom; they do not hide it." Here in America, Gay Pride "parades" are held all over the country, where they openly display their wickedness, flaunting their sin before God and man. This passage from Isaiah gives us some insight into the depth of wickedness that Sodom and Gomorrah had sunk. This is not homophobia, but a clarion call for national repentance to avoid national destruction. Open homosexuality is an explicit biblical sign of a nation headed for collapse. Again, these are not my words—they're God's!

Social Decline

America's social decline was so powerfully articulated in the HBO series *Newsroom*, where the principal character, news anchor Will McAvoy, gives his critical assessment of America after being asked, "What makes America the greatest country in the World?" His answer:

"…there's absolutely no evidence to support the statement that we're the greatest country in the world. We're seventh in literacy, twenty-seventh in math, twenty-second in science, forty-ninth in life expectancy, 178th in infant mortality, third in median household income, number four in labor force and number four in exports. We lead the world in only three categories: Number of incarcerated citizens per capita, number of adults who believe angels are real, and defense spending where we spend more than the next twenty-six countries combined, twenty-five of whom are allies….

It sure used to be. We stood up for what was right. We fought for moral reasons. We passed laws, struck down laws for moral reasons. We waged wars on poverty, not poor people. We sacrificed, we cared about our neighbors, we put our money where our mouths were and we never beat our chests. We built great big things, made ungodly technological advances, explored the universe, cured diseases, and cultivated the world's greatest artists and the world's greatest economy. We reached for the stars, acted like men, we aspired to intelligence, we didn't belittle it, it didn't make us feel inferior. We didn't identify ourselves by who we voted for in the last election and we didn't scare so easy. We were able to be all these things and do all these things because we were informed, by great men, men who were revered. First step in solving any problem

> is recognizing there is one. America is not the greatest country in the world anymore."[42]

Though what's stated above is fictional, the assessment, in general, is accurate. The glory and prestige of America have faded. However, I differ from the character McAvory's assessment as to the cause of America's decline. America has rejected the very God that made her the greatest among the nations. Psalm 9:17 states, "the wicked shall be turned into hell, *and* all the nations that forget God." This is a significant passage because it doesn't say the nations *that do not know God;* that may actually be preferred rather than to have known God and *forget* Him! Here we have an act of national volition, a pervasive social consciousness of a society that rejects God's authority and the restraints of His moral law. One of the greatest consequences from a decline in God's moral law is inevitable social decline. When a nation turns its back on God, corruption, confusion, and chaos follow closely in its wake. Without any moral absolutes, there are no boundaries, and people live as if they were in the times of the Judges where "every man did what was right in his own eyes." Where there is a total breakdown of centralized government, there is anarchy.

In 2 Timothy 3, Paul, two thousand years ago, gives us insight into today's world and the perilous times that are now upon us.

> But know this, that in the last days perilous times will come: For men will be lovers of themselves, lovers of money, boasters, proud, blasphemers, disobedient to parents, unthankful, unholy, unloving, unforgiving, slanderers,

> without self-control, brutal, despisers of good, traitors, headstrong, haughty, lovers of pleasure rather than lovers of God, having a form of godliness but denying its power.
>
> 2 Timothy 3:1-5, NKJV

Though this Scripture is speaking of the world in general, America certainly cannot be removed from the equation. Certainly, this passage includes all of the violence and lawlessness that we see in our society today.

The Whole World is Watching

During the 1968 Democratic Convention in Chicago, as protesters were being beaten and tear-gassed by Chicago police riot squads, 10,000 protesters chanted this phrase, "The whole world is watching," as their blood flowed in the streets. Camera crews from around the country captured this historic political embarrassment showing how dirty and dangerous American politics can really be. Chicago Mayor Richard J. Daley, who previously had boasted that "we know how to throw a national convention," sent thousands of police armed in riot gear and night sticks to "control the mob," which only exacerbated the situation that ignited the riot. Eighty-three million viewers watched as Chicago police "controlled" the situation through brute force, leaving an ugly scar on the American political consciousness.

The essence of "the whole world is watching" mantra reinforces the idea that the world sees how ugly America "the beautiful" can really be. It underscores the contradiction of a nation that prides itself as being the champion for human rights, when in fact the opposite is true for millions of African Americans, Hispanics, women, and other ethnic and social groups.

In the years 2012 through 2015, America has been turned upside down with massive protests and riots over the killing of unarmed black men and youth. Protest in multiple cities around the country ensued after the killing of Trayvon Martin in Sanford, Florida, where protesters wore hoodies, the same as Trayvon wore the night he was murdered.

Horrific riots, reminiscent of the Los Angeles Rodney King riots of 1992, broke out in Ferguson, Missouri, where Michael Brown, unarmed and hands up, was killed and the grand jury found no reason to charge Officer Darren Wilson for wrongful death. Destructive riots broke out in Baltimore after the killing of Freddie Gray, another unarmed black man arrested for no apparent reason who ended up with a severed spinal cord and a crushed larynx. In Chicago, 17-year-old Laquan McDonald was shot sixteen times, fourteen as he laid helplessly on the ground, by a Chicago, police officer. The dash-cam video release of the shooting and the subsequent cover-up that ensued after the incident sparked national and international outrage and led to a Justice Department investigation concerning corruption in the Chicago Police Department.

Understanding that not all law enforcement is bad, the numbers of violent atrocities committed by law enforcement and in many cases backed by the courts against minorities and the poor, have millions in an uproar.

There is much social unrest in America. Relations between the races are at an all-time low while violence and corruption are at an all-time high. Mass murders, deranged individuals shooting up malls, schools, theaters, and churches sporadically surface so that there is no way to predict when psychos will strike next. American diplomats across the globe are telling everyone else how they should have better human rights, while the world community stands back and looks with a raised eyebrow at America's hypocrisy as social injustices happen with alarming regularity.

Nations around the world see us as a big hypocrite lecturing them on human rights while unarmed black youth are being murdered by police without any repercussions from a judicial system and prosecutors who typically do not indict police. We have more incarcerated people than any other country in the world, fueled by a school-to-prison pipeline that feeds an increasingly privatized prison industry. Even worse, many of those on death row are innocent but were sentenced by overzealous prosecutors more interested in a conviction rather than the truth. Since 1993, evidence has overturned the death sentences of 155 inmates.[43] Of course this does not include the thousands of wrongly convicted with lesser sentences. Many corrupt police officers such as convicted cop Jon Burge, an infamous Chicago detective who tortured confessions out of countless blacks, is evidence of a police and court system that is often blind when it comes to justice for blacks. African Americans disproportionately make up the largest percentage of incarcerated people out of any group in America.

On the other hand, inner city crime is off the chain, as minority youth often kill each other in the streets in one of the worst sprees of bloodletting the nation has ever seen. However, whereas black-on-black crimes are reported in the news, 80 percent of all murders among whites in America are committed by other whites, a statistic rarely reported. America by far is one of the most violent "civilized" countries in the world.

During the war in Afghanistan, over 1,850 American casualties occurred due to hostile actions from 2001 to 2015. However, in 2013 there were 14,196 murders in the United States. That is more than seven times the military casualties that occurred in a war zone during a 14-year period, as opposed to one year in America.

America parades around the world touting that foreign governments should conduct free and open elections, while America is involved in a wave of voter suppression laws that would disenfranchise millions of registered minority voters, while some are working feverishly to undo the benefits of the Civil Rights and Voting Rights Acts. America spends billions of dollars on foreign aid to other countries while many of America's poor urban and rural areas have underperforming and inadequately equipped schools. The United States has thousands of miles of highways and an alarming number of bridges that need critical repair. We will send money to feed the hungry in other countries but will not fund hot-lunch programs for needy children here at home.

America claims to be the upholder of peace around the world, while our government is the largest exporter of military arms in the world. Not to mention the fact that the State Department cooked up an excuse to invade Iraq over weapons of mass destruction when our government knew they did not exist. Therefore, the purpose to get Saddam Hussein was just a cover-up so we could establish military bases in Iraq. Of course, this plan backfired, and now ISIS has filled in the Iraq power void.

What is mentioned here is the tip of the iceberg, but it underscores the fact that the "whole world is watching." The global community hears America say one thing, but so many times sees her do something different. This is how a great nation becomes "small" in the eyes of its neighbors, allies, and enemies. It is not the size of its military or amount of money in its banks, but it is the economic, moral, and social decline that causes it to become small.

Military Decline

In June 1974, I joined the United States Navy. After boot camp, my first tour of duty was to serve on the *U.S.S. England*, a guided-missile cruiser stationed at the 32nd Street Naval Station in San Diego, California. My first commanding officer was Captain John M. Poindexter, a nuclear physicist, who rose quickly through the ranks to become a Vice Admiral, and President Reagan's National Security Advisor. At the time, the Navy's whole philosophy was to patrol the high seas to ensure that the shipping lanes remained free and to keep a strong military presence in the oceans around the world, particularly in regions where American interests were at stake.

The number one concern of the Navy that was and still holds true to this day is what the Soviet Union was doing. The Soviets, or since the breakup of the Soviet Union or USSR, Russia, had about the only navy in the world that could go toe-to-toe with America. Though the Soviet navy was not as advanced as ours, they were a close second, and actually surpassed the United States numerically, when it came to the number of cruisers, destroyers, and submarines. Where they lacked in technology, they made up in numbers. There was constant back and forth between the two nations during the period known as the Cold War. These two nations, though they did not necessarily like or trust one another, certainly had a great deal of respect for one another. Each nation had the military armament, both offensive and defensive, to launch a catastrophic nuclear attack assuring that, in such an exchange, assured mutual destruction for both would be inevitable. We designed weapons systems to counter theirs and vice versa. That's what always kept either side from "pushing the button" and starting a nuclear war.

For a long time after World War II, American military power and presence was the greatest in the world. We, through our advanced technology, dropped nuclear bombs on Japan, forcing them to surrender, which in turn negated the necessity of a bloody American invasion. The world was in absolute shock at America's new, incredibly destructive weapon. At this point, no one dared test America's resolve to win a fight. No other nation in the world has ever used nuclear weapons on a foreign country since. For a time, America stood alone as the single most powerful nation in the world. This strategic advantage gave us a great deal of clout both militarily and politically.

However, today that is not the case, partly because military technology has been proliferated with all sorts of armament that has made the world a much more dangerous place. For example, one of America's chief allies in the Middle East was Iran. Iran had an American-backed political regime through its ruler Mohammad Reza Pahlavi, the Shah of Iran, who came to power during the American and British-backed *coup d'état* that placed him in power in 1953. The Shah was favorable toward American and British oil companies and their strategic oil interests. However, a puppet regime ruling in Iran did not sit well with many of Iran's religious leaders and citizens, particularly since America backed Israel. As it turned out, this was a political disaster waiting to happen—and it did—when the Shah was overthrown on February 11, 1979.

While stationed in San Diego during the mid-1970s, I remember having a conversation with Iranian sailors who were there training at the Naval Training Center. They didn't seem to like being in America, and I distinctly remember they had a negative attitude and gave the impression that they didn't like Americans either. Nevertheless, the fact that they were there was an indication of the type of close relationship the U.S. once had with Iran. We trained their navy, sold them advanced weaponry like Spruance-class destroyers and F-14 fighter jets. However, none of that made a difference when Ayatollah Khomeini, the founder of the Islamic Republic, rose up against the Shah's regime and led a successful revolution against the Shah, declaring Iran to be an Islamic Republic. The U.S. Embassy was then seized, and fifty-two embassy workers were taken hostage in a standoff between the United States and Iran that lasted for 444 days.

On April 24, 1980, I was in the Indian Ocean on a naval supply ship, the *U.S.S. Mars*, that was part of the *U.S.S. Nimitz* task force that launched the ill-fated rescue attempt to free the Iranian hostages. As the *Mars* pulled alongside the *Nimitz* to transfer supplies, I remember seeing in one of the *Nimitz*'s hanger bays the H-53 helicopters that would be used in the rescue attempt. I also remember the unfortunate day the news broke about those helicopters crashing and the soldiers dying in the failed rescue attempt. The most advanced military in the world bumbled this operation, which turned out to be the nail in the coffin for the Jimmy Carter presidency.

I bring all of this up because it is indicative of the many failures of American foreign policy, which have caused our allies and enemies to see us as a country that no longer has the capability to protect itself, to back up its foreign policy or protect its allies' interests.

America has been involved in too many fights that it has not been able to win. The Korean Conflict ended in a stalemate between North and South Korea that lasts to this day. Then, of course, there was the Vietnam War, where, after about ten years of fighting, we had to pull out without a win. There was the invasion of Iraq with the intention of setting up a democratic government and training and building up Iraq forces so they could govern themselves. Once again, that turned out to be a failure, with parts of the country now under ISIS control. After fourteen years of being bogged down in Afghanistan, nothing has changed for the better there either. With all the lives, hardware, billions of dollars, and the lost credibility, America is seen around the world as a giant whose bark is worse than its bite. With all of its technological power, America cannot stop ISIS, who sees America as a nation that will launch a missile or send a drone from far away, but who does not want to commit to having boots on the ground.

In many of these hotspots around the world, unless you have boots on the ground there is no way to win. And even if you put boots on the ground, implementing a good exit strategy as well as a strategy to win can be evasive in fluid military campaigns. Americans have grown weary of war and disapprove of sending our soldiers to die in battle in regions of the world that will eventually turn against us.

Recently President Obama drew the proverbial line in the sand concerning Syrian President Bashar al-Assad (whose birthday, ironically, is September 11th) using chemical weapons on the rebels behind the uprising against the Assad regime. The president stated:

> "We have communicated in no uncertain terms with every player in the region that's a red line for us and that there would be enormous consequences if we start seeing movement on the chemical weapons front or the use of chemical weapons," he said. "That would change my calculations significantly."[44]

As we all know, the Assad regime did, in fact, use chemical weapons and no military action was taken by the United States. As a result, this turned out to be a credibility nightmare because the President backed himself into a corner. The Assad regime as well as many antagonists in the region knew that America would not be willing to send troops into Syria, which gave Assad the leverage he needed to call the President's bluff. As long as America keeps drawing "lines in the sand," taking a step backward every time she does, these despots are going to keep committing atrocities. Now Russia has sent military support and weaponry into Syria to help defend itself against ISIS—so they claim.

The world knows that America's options are limited and that it cannot back up all of its rhetoric. This has seriously damaged our image around the world. It has hurt our credibility and relationship with our allies. Obadiah warns, "All your allies will force you to the border; your friends will deceive and overpower you; those who eat your bread will set a trap for you, but you will not detect it" (Obadiah

1:7, NIV 2011). Though America will act unilaterally, it cannot solve every problem in the world with a drone or a cruise missile. Additionally, America does not have the capability to put out all of the world's fires. If they send troops, how long will they stay? If they send cruise missiles and drones, in the end how effective will that be? If they send weapons and financial support to resistance fighters, that too could backfire, as it did in Afghanistan when the CIA backed the rebels' fight to expel the Russians. What resulted from that? Osama bin Laden and the al-Qaeda we know today.

To sum it all up, America has been made "small among the nations." We are no longer the world's moral or military authority. Frankly, given the challenges of the 21st century, our military would be hard pressed to execute our national strategy. The readiness of our Army is the worst it has been any time in the history of the United States. Our Air Force is operating on fewer and older aircraft since its creation during WWII. Our Navy has fewer ships while the military budgets continue to be cut. All of these aspects of military decline are happening in the context of an increasingly volatile world where America's foreign policies are contested and our enemies are emboldened.

On the other hand, America is further weakened by its hypocrisies abroad by responding only to "favorable" international crisis while turning a blind eye to others. For example, we will turn our backs on genocide in Rwanda, a black African nation with no strategic interests to

America, where millions were slaughtered, but open our borders to thousands of Syrian refugees fleeing the war with ISIS in Syria. We put great effort into preventing the Iranians from developing nuclear weapons, but were powerless to stop the North Koreans from obtaining and exploding theirs. That's because short of a preemptive nuclear strike, or an out-of-the-question invasion, there is nothing America can do to North Korea that they haven't already done to stop them. You never hear about America using military options to stop North Korea. This is why North Korea's leader, Kim Jong-un, openly defies America because they can fight back. Having nuclear weapons is a game changer.

When the North Korean's hacked Sony's computers, and threatened retribution over the release of the movie *The Interview*, the government could not give enough reassurance for the public's safety, consequently, theaters refused to show the film. A foreign government backed down a major U.S. corporation on our soil! Granted, bombing a nation over for cyber crimes may not be an option—but that's the point! This is a new day, where America no longer has all the strategic advantages. All of this clearly accentuates Obadiah's prophecy, "See, I will make you small among the nations..." (Ob. 1:2, NIV).

Chapter 5
Thou Art Greatly Despised

The next aspect of Obadiah's prophecy is "thou art greatly despised." Typically, we Americans see ourselves in a completely different light than other nations around the world. When comparing ourselves to other nations, we see ourselves as prestigious, powerful, and privileged. We have a very strong sense of "American pride." From our vantage point, obviously there is nothing wrong with that, because America is the world's foremost superpower. However, this aspect of Obadiah's prophecy to the Edomites, once again, aligns with modern-day America. You see, it is not really about how we see ourselves as a nation, but it's about how the world sees and really feels about America. We see ourselves as "blessed and have it made." But how does the world really feel about America? As it was with the Edomites, so it is with America, "we are greatly despised." The question is, why?

From our sense of self-worth, we see ourselves as a nation that stands up for righteousness around the world. It is similar to the intro of the popular 1950-60s weekly television program *Superman*, where the program's announcer would say that Supermen stood for "truth, justice, and the American way." This line was stated as Superman posed in front of a waving American flag. Unfortunately, "the American way" during the 1950s was not being realized for millions of African Americans. The United States was still in the clutches of Jim Crow laws; separate but equal and legalized systemic racial prejudice were still in effect where African Americans did not have the right to vote, could not attend certain schools, were relegated to holding only subservient jobs, could not eat at certain restaurants, or stay in certain hotels. They could not utilize public facilities such as restrooms that whites used, nor drink from the same water fountains as whites. These were blatant contradictions to what America said it stood for, and represented how it actually treated its own citizens. Obviously, there was some hypocrisy with *truth, justice* and *America's way*.

During his interview with Charlie Rose on *60 Minutes* on September 25, 2015, Russian President Vladimir Putin retorted to one of Rose's questions about human rights in Russia by bringing up Ferguson, Missouri, and the killing of Michael Brown. He also mentioned America's involvement in the ousting of Ukraine's former president Viktor Yanukovych, who was forced to flee to Russia in 2014. Though officially the United States denies any involvement, Putin asserted, "I know this for sure." To others,

America's hypocrisy is obvious no matter how much it is denied. The fact is, people typically despise hypocrites.

Americans have been deluded by our own sense of prestige and power just as were the ancient Edomites. As covered previously, the ancient Edomites controlled the main trade routes that passed through their country. They were rich in natural resources. They had the advantage of natural fortification, being situated high in a rocky, mountainous region making them feel that they were impervious to invasion or attack. In a similar sense, America is rich with natural and agricultural resources. We are the key player in international economics and trade because the U.S. dollar is the foremost international reserve currency. We have the world's foremost military, and we are strategically located, being separated from the rest of world by two great oceans (the Atlantic on the east and the Pacific on the west). On our northern and southern borders, we have friendly relationships with Canada and Mexico, respectively.

We have an open democratic society with a bill of rights for our citizens. We are a capitalist society where it is possible for anyone to become rich and powerful. Anyone can attend any church they choose or attend no church at all. You can own real estate and land. You can go to good schools and become beneficiaries of equal justice under the law. These are just a few enviable traits about America. In comparison to other countries on earth, the United States is certainly the place to be.

However, there is a duality to this reality. There is a flip side to the proverbial American coin. The same things that make this a great nation are the same things that also make this nation despised by others. Everyone wants to knock down and replace the king of the hill. Once you make it to the top, you have to fight to stay there. And it's how you fight to stay on top that makes all the difference in the world.

I mentioned briefly that in 1974, at the age of 17, I joined the United States Navy. Being stationed on the West Coast, by the time I had turned 21, I had been to several countries. Our ship visited the typical countries on the Westpac (naval term for Western Pacific) route: Japan, Guam, Korea, the Philippines, Thailand, Taiwan, Hong Kong, Diego Garcia, Oman, and other countries such as Canada, and Mexico. The open exposure to those parts of the world outside the United States was an eye opener. I've never thought of the world the same as I did prior to stepping foot on foreign soil.

While onboard the ship, the commanding officer would always brief us on the countries that we were visiting. We would be told that "not every place was a safe place to go," because all of the countries where we visited had some anti-American sentiments. I found this to be true during my first visit to the Philippines. The United States had two main bases in the Philippines, Clark Air Force Base and Subic Bay Naval Base. Both bases brought millions of dollars to those local economies. Many of the towns surrounding the bases were set up to cater to the thousands of American service members. Though the indigenous people who made a living off the military loved our money and tolerated our typical obnoxious behavior, a little farther out from those hospitable towns were those who despised our presence.

I recall a sailor getting into an argument with one of the Filipino bar girls (Olongapo City, the town immediately outside the naval base, had hundreds of bars for the sailors). All of these establishments were there to cater to the revelry of the American military. Each bar had paid prostitutes that worked as bar girls, and sailors could pay about 30 or 40 pesos (less than $10 U.S.) to buy them out of the bar and take them home. Young women from all over the Philippines came there to make money to support their families by servicing the Americans. Of course, the sailors loved it, but underneath all the money and carousal, there was disdain boiling under the surface over the American exploitation of Filipinos. Granted, though the bar owners and Olongapo City officials were equally culpable, it's still exploitation.

I recall a sailor asking, "Why do you Filipinos prostitute yourselves out like this" (as if the sailor was any better than she was). Of course, she sharply retorted that he had no right to judge her or her people. Clearly, the sailor had struck a nerve—that's the problem. Americans think they are so much better than everyone else that even when we don't realize it, we carry this air of "I am a privileged American." So, many countries dislike Americans, but love our money.

Eventually, the American-backed Marcos dictatorship that ruled in the Philippines was overthrown, and the Marcos family was forced to flee, with millions of dollars of the Philippines' money. Needless to say, once Marcos was deposed, in the following years those bases were closed. Damage from a volcano closed Clark Air Force base, and Subic Bay Naval Base was shut down. Though many wanted the bases to stay open, others wanted them closed because they represented shameful exploitation of the Filipino people.

A New York Times article observed:

> "... the Philippine Senate rejected the treaty in September after an impassioned debate in which the American military presence was assailed as a vestige of colonialism and an affront to Philippine sovereignty."[45]

Currently, there are over 140 American bases around the world where our military has strategic interests. In those same countries, once you get farther out from the military bases, you will find out how people really feel about a foreign military being stationed in their country. We stage our bases, our planes, our soldiers, our missiles in someone else's backyard, exploiting their country for our political and strategic purposes. That scenario, though mutually beneficial, at certain levels breeds discontent amongst the citizenry.

How many foreign military bases are in America? None. Do Americans have to put up with the foreign soldiers and sailors walking our streets and through our communities, corrupting our children and disrespecting our way of life? No! I distinctly remember when I was in Yokosuka, Japan, and some of my fellow sailors had the nerve to wear a T-shirt that stated, *Hiroshima, Nagasaki, boom, boom, boom*, featuring a mushroom cloud in the background. What audacity! It made me cringe, and it also got them beaten within an inch of their lives. Through the arrogance of believing themselves to be superior, these naïve young men in their twenties almost left Japan in a casket. Of course, these are not the actions of all Americans who travel abroad. The difference is these were military personnel, not tourists. These sailors were representatives of the United States government. The idea of the "truth, justice and the American way," self-proclaimed, police of the world role is deplorable to many of the world's citizens, who see all the American discord going on in our own country. We are in no position to be telling anyone else what to do.

America promotes itself as being a peaceful nation and feeds its population with the idea that we are the "good guys," when in reality the U.S. is one of the most violent industrialized nations in the world. America claims to be a world leader in human rights, yet with only five percent of the world's population consumes the most illicit drugs of any nation on earth. America has twenty-five percent of the world's incarcerated population. Even America's drug enforcement laws unfairly target African Americans and other minorities. For example, powder cocaine penalties are much lighter than crack cocaine penalties.

The devastation that crack caused in urban areas led to the Congressional Black Caucus pressing the CIA about their involvement in the sales proliferation of crack cocaine in the black communities in Los Angeles during the 1980s. The Iran-Contra scandal had much to do with the cocaine traffic in many urban areas throughout the country, but primarily it started in the black communities of the Los Angeles area. After letting these drugs in, the government imposed stricter sentencing guidelines for crack users, knowing full well that the government was partly to blame for the crack epidemic. Where are the human rights in that?

Congress passed a weapons embargo on Iran and would not approve funding to be allocated to the Contras in Nicaragua, because of their affiliation with the drug cartels. However, with the assistance of the CIA, North's and Poindexter's scheme to circumvent congressional prohibitions involved siphoning profits from massive cocaine sales that were allowed to flood Los Angeles and other U.S. cities. It was this insidious pipeline from Nicaragua to Los Angeles that led to the crack epidemic that ravished inner-city communities throughout America. Senator John Kerry's committee found the following:

> "It is clear that individuals who provided support for the Contras were involved in drug trafficking, the supply network of the Contras was used by drug trafficking organizations, and elements of the Contras themselves knowingly received financial and material assistance from drug traffickers."[46]

Many continue to debate the level of the CIA's involvement, and of course the agency denies it. In any case, at the very least, they did nothing to stop the flow into the United States nor stop the money from flowing out. This same money went to buy weapons for the Contras (a revolutionary group backed by the CIA to overthrow the Sandinistas, a communist regime in Nicaragua). Secondly, these funds also went to purchase weapons for the Iranians for their help in releasing Americans being held hostage in Lebanon. This is known as the "*weapons for hostages scandal*."

My former commanding officer of the *USS England*, Vice Admiral John Poindexter and his aide Colonel Oliver North were the front men for the Reagan administration. The great hypocrisy was that this was at the height of Reagan's "War on Drugs," and Nancy Reagan's "Just Say No" campaign. These actions were both illegal and immoral. Poindexter and North were both convicted, but neither served any time. Ironically, a black person caught with a bag of crack could go to jail for 10 years or more. Where is the justice or human rights in that?

Our prisons are filled with non-violent, predominately black and Hispanic drug offenders who need help, not incarceration. But the "human rights champion" of the world, the United States, would rather spend more money on prisons than on schools, better education, job training, drug rehabilitation, and community development. The whole world sees what America has not done with its own people, while it tries to dictate to other countries what they should be doing with theirs. This kind of hypocrisy is the reason we are greatly despised.

The following are nations where CIA-backed coups, not including multiple military campaigns, were conducted: Iran, 1953; Guatemala, 1954; the Congo, 1960; the Dominican Republic, 1961; South Viet Nam, 1963; Brazil, 1964; and Chile, 1973. However, *Salon.com* lists thirty-five nations where the CIA backed fascists, drug lords, and terrorists.[47] Here are just a few: Afghanistan, 1980s; Albania (between 1948 and 1953); Argentina, 1976, Cuba (the U.S.-backed Batista dictatorship was overthrown by Fidel Castro, and years later President Kennedy was ill-advised by military officials to launch the Cuban invasion known as the Bay of Pigs, which ended up an embarrassing defeat); El Salvador, 1980s; Haiti, 1990; Honduras, 2009; Indonesia, 1965. In Iraq in 1958—"after the British-backed monarchy was overthrown by General Abdul Qasim, the CIA hired a 22-year-old Iraqi named Saddam Hussein to assassinate the new president. Hussein and his gang botched the job and he fled to Lebanon, wounded in the leg by one of his companions. The CIA rented him an apartment in Beirut and then moved him to Cairo, where he was paid as an agent of Egyptian intelligence and was a frequent visitor at the U.S. Embassy." Finally, Panama, was invaded by America to capture President Noriega, a well-known CIA-backed drug dealer. President George H.W. Bush laid out four reasons for invading Panama, one of course on the basis of "defending human rights and democracy." Noriega was a CIA operative while Bush was the director of the CIA, and the former was in direct contact with Bush. The CIA was well aware that Noriega was a drug kingpin whom they were keeping in power.

Much of this information (and there is a lot more) has been declassified and made available. The American public, while we are living comfortably in our nice homes with paved streets and manicured lawns, eating pizza and hot dogs, watching our favorite game shows and sports teams, have no idea of the dirty, covert operations hatched by our country around the world. We are on the sending end of these operations. We only know what we hear from our media outlets. In other words, we only know what they want us to know about what's really going on. However, try being on the receiving end of all this. What if foreign governments were trying to overthrow the American government, launch a coup to put in a puppet regime here in America? Wouldn't we feel the same disdain for them as they undoubtedly feel for us?

Maybe many of these things had to be done, such as the killing of Osama bin Laden in Pakistan. Our military carried out a search and destroy mission in a sovereign nation without their permission. It's what we had to do, right? But at the same time, how do you think it made the Pakistanis feel? Or, would we say, "Who cares?" That's the point, *they* care. The Pakistanis were on the receiving end of a raid that left several dead, while we cheered and applauded the announcement! They were outraged because their sovereignty was violated. What is often good for Americans has adverse effects and consequences for other nations. Am I suggesting that America should not have acted on Osama bin Laden? Of course not. Are there justifications, at least from our point of view, for many of our covert and overt actions? Yes. All I am saying is there are two sides to those coins. Since we are the great world superpower, we see these actions from our elevated perspective, as did the Edomites, but the rest of the world does not have that same perspective.

For example, look at all the casualties of war; the drone strikes, and misplaced smart bombs that hit innocent, non-combatant targets where our military has accidentally killed foreign nationals. What's our response to this? Do we say, "Oops, our bad." Or, "We send our condolences over the loss of your loved ones, but it's for a good cause."

Americans don't have to live with the threat of another nation's air force dropping bombs on our cities. We dole that out to others, but we don't have to take it. In a most recent event, once again, the U.S. military hit the wrong target and bombed a hospital run by Doctors Without Borders in the Afghan city of Kunduz, on October 3, 2015, killing 30 innocent people and injuring many others. Initial reports indicated that the hospital was badly damaged. Hospital officials insisted "the hospital location was well known, and was the only operating hospital in Kunduz…we shared extensively the locations of this hospital with all warring parties in Afghanistan."[48]

When you are a world leader, being envied and disliked goes along with the territory; but some of the disdain we receive is deserved. In cases like these, "We send our sincerest apologies and condolences...," just doesn't cut it. As Obadiah said to the Edomites, "I have made the small among the nations, thou art greatly despised…" (Obadiah 1:3 KJV), so it is with America.

Chapter 6
The Pride of Your Heart Has Deceived You

If there is one characteristic of an individual, a ruler, or nation that displeases God, it would be the sin of pride. As our thematic text reveals, pride is powerfully deceptive. Pride will make you think you are better than who you *really* are, smarter and stronger than you *actually* are, and more self-sufficient than you *truly* are. The irony about pride is, at the center of the word *pride* is "I."

In 1 Timothy 3:6, the apostle writes: "…lest being puffed up with pride he fall into the *same* condemnation as the devil." Though this passage is in reference to not promoting too quickly a newly converted individual into a position of church leadership, there are underlying principles here that apply universally. Once individuals are exalted in pride, they come under the same condemnation or judgment, as did Satan. The following passage tells us exactly what happened to Satan. Isaiah 14:12-15, NKJV reads:

> *How* you are fallen from heaven, O Lucifer, son of the morning! How you are cut down to the ground, You who weakened the nations! For you have said in your heart: 'I will ascend into heaven, I will exalt my throne above the stars of God; I will also sit on the mount of the congregation on the farthest sides of the north; I will ascend above the heights of the clouds, I will be like the Most High.' Yet you shall be brought down to Sheol, To the lowest depths of the pit.

As we stated in the opening of this chapter, at the center of pride is "I." That's exactly what we see here with Satan. Clearly, Satan fell because he had an "I" problem. The five "I will" statements that sealed his fate were: *I will* ascend into heaven, *I will* exalt my throne above the stars of God, *I will* also sit on the mount of the congregation on the farthest sides of the north, *I will* ascend above the heights of the clouds, *I will* be like the Most High.

This part of Obadiah's prophecy in verse 3 that I believe correlates to the United States focuses on national pride. Pride makes you arrogant. Pride makes a nation think the rest of the world likes, or fears it. Pride makes a nation think that since it has resources it is self-sufficient. National pride and arrogance make a government think that it is invincible and can defeat any foe and be defeated by none. Pride makes a country believe everyone else in the world is wrong, but everything it does is right. Pride causes a nation to justify its mistakes and mitigate its hypocrisies, while being critical and condemning others. But the worst of all is that pride deludes a nation that once acknowledged

God to think that it can act or even exist independently of God. This was Satan's great sin. This was also King Nebuchadnezzar's sin. He attempted to displace God by saying, "This is the great Babylon that I have built." Even after God warned him not to ever say that again, he sought to defy God and was immediately judged.

Whether it is the pride of people or the pride of nations, pride ultimately leads to destruction. Proverbs tells us, "Pride goes before destruction…." Prideful nations quickly become blinded to their true inability and actual reliance on God, to opt for the false impression of self-sufficiency. It is reminiscent of the spider that trusts in the integrity of its web. To the spider, it is well built and anchored. To the spider, it's strong, when in reality, it's nothing. Here is what God says: "Such is the destiny of all who forget God; so perishes the hope of the godless. What they trust in is fragile; what they rely on is a spider's web. They lean on the web, but it gives way; they cling to it, but it does not hold" (Job 8:13-15, NIV 2011).

Isaiah has similar sentiments when he writes: "Before him all the nations are as nothing; they are regarded by him as worthless and less than nothing" (Isaiah 40:17, NIV 2011). Therefore, the nation that is lifted up in pride has been deceived and mistakenly believes that it no longer needs to rely on or even acknowledge God. Unfortunately, this is what is happening to America. It was a nation that once cherished the idea of being "one nation under God." However, in past decades, through the efforts of secular humanists, agnostics, and atheists, America has been steered in an untoward direction that positions herself from being *away* from God as opposed to being *under* God.

An interesting fact about the Edomites is that they were from a rich history, a lineage that inherited the blessings of Abraham. Esau, being the grandson of Abraham and the favorite son of Isaac, was certainly in line for God's blessing and favor; however, he counted his birthright as nothing, trading it for a bowl of red soup. In a like manner, America was founded on principles that acknowledged the God of the Bible. Due to the Constitution, America was a land where people could have religious freedom. Therefore, with freedom and opportunity before them, people came from all over the world to America's fertile shores. Free to worship God and not be forced to worship according to restrictions placed on it by a state-sponsored religion, America embraced those who sought a better life in a promising new land that God would use as a platform to transform the entire world.

In the *Introduction*, we covered how Paul's appeal on Mars Hill to the Greek philosophers brought out a point that is important to reiterate here. It is God who foreordains when and where the people of the earth shall live, and with the stated purpose that people might seek after Him and find Him (see Acts 17:26-27). All that live in America were chosen to be here, from the Native Americans first, to the Europeans, the Africans, the Asians, those from the Middle East to the farthest regions of the world. We are all part of this great American project.

God has used America to be the platform to revolutionize the world. Think of all the inventions, innovations, and industries that have come out of this country since the Industrial Revolution and beyond. According to *Encyclopedia Britannica's Greatest Inventions*, 161 of the world's greatest 325 inventions came from the United States. Certainly, the world is a much better place because of the good that has come out of America.

However, the crack in America's foundation in recent past decades has been the concept of *separation of church and state*. This phrase used by Thomas Jefferson, also referred to as "the wall of separation of church and state," dealt with *the establishment* and the *free exercise* clause, of the First Amendment. Thomas Jefferson wrote, "I contemplate with sovereign reverence that act of the whole American people which declared that their legislature should 'make no law respecting an establishment of religion, or prohibiting the free exercise thereof,' thus building a wall of separation between Church and State."[49] Many see Jefferson's words as the legal basis for the government not to impede the establishment or growth of the Church here in America. However, separation of church and state has been a two-edged sword that in recent decades has become the basis for attacking the very freedoms that the Church has always exercised and enjoyed. Contemporary usage of the separation clause that in the past has favored *freedom of religion* in key court cases now supports a *freedom from religion* interpretation as moral and immoral philosophies clash.

As the Scriptures declare, "Through the blessing of the upright a city is exalted, but by the mouth of the wicked it is destroyed." "Righteousness exalts a nation, but sin condemns any people." (Proverbs 11:11;14:34, NIV). Righteousness (by biblical standards, not secular humanist standards) is what elevates a nation. The sad issue for America is, our Constitution makes the pursuit of religion a protected right, but it also makes the pursuit of wickedness and debauchery a protected right as well. We have now come to a point in America where the two are not coexisting peacefully. Just as Jacob and Esau could not coexist peacefully, even in their mother's womb (see Genesis 25:22-23), so it is with morality and immorality, light and darkness, the kingdom of God and the kingdom of Satan, the religious and the secular.

In John 3:19-20, the Bible declares:

> This is the verdict: Light has come into the world, but people loved darkness instead of light because their deeds were evil. Everyone who does evil hates the light, and will not come into the light for fear that their deeds will be exposed. NIV 2011

As this Scripture teaches, wickedness hates the light, because it exposes its evil intentions. This is at the center of why the world hates the God of the Bible. It is also why the Church in America is so hated by the secular society, because in Christ's stead, we (the Church) are the light of the world. The Church is the beacon of moral light that exposes and confronts the wickedness of this nation. As the nation drifts farther away from God, secular political, legal, educational forces have tipped the scales of justice in favor of a legal interpretation of the freedom and establishment clauses to a much more liberal interpretation of the Constitution concerning religious verses secular rights.

In our public schools, you can teach evolution as "established" fact (a theory that denies the existence of God, or God's role in creation) in public schools. You also have school curriculums that promote same-sex relationships such as books depicting two mommies or two daddies. On the other hand, secularist school administrations will suspend a child for reading his Bible, not in class but during recess! This occurred in July 2015 in Plainview, Texas.[50] The school's position was that the boy had been warned several times about "practicing religion." However, he wasn't practicing religion; he was reading the Bible! He wasn't baptizing, or proselytizing; he was reading his Bible. When you study history, is that called "practicing history"? No, of course not. This is the perfect example of how the anti-God movement has morphed *freedom of religion* into *freedom from religion*.

Secularists enjoy their right to express their freedom from anything religious, while denying a middle-school youth his right to practice his freedom to read his Bible. These unjust incidents of the denial of religious freedom are committed under the guise of separation of church and state. Anti-God philosophies are promoted when and wherever they please, but for a child to even open a Bible during school hours is an offense worthy of being expelled. I truly believe that this was not what the framers of the Constitution had in mind with the concept of separation of church and state.

Once the American court system adjudicated God out of the classroom, out of the public arenas, basically making God the enemy of the state, by way of separation, it opened the door for persecution in every quarter of society, against those who dare to publicly stand up for their faith. Freedom from religion is a position preferred by a secular society and government. With that being the case, the nation that was once "under God" has now elevated human rights above God's moral authority, even denying His very existence in all public governmental arenas. This is only a part of the many ways that this nation has forgotten God. Through the courts and legislative processes God has been voted out, and therefore wickedness prevails—though not ultimately.

When a nation rejects God, it is only left to trust in itself. Its military, political, and economic powers are the basis in which it stands and interacts with the global community. Here is where pride raises its ugly head. Pride says: We are sovereign, we are self-sufficient, were are powerful, and undefeatable. Pride says, "We don't recognize the Bible as authoritative. Therefore, we will not have God or the Bible rule over us." "America the beautiful was built by our own hands without any help from God." But a nation that forgets and rejects God is headed for destruction and shall reap the bitter fruit sprouting from the seeds of pride planted deep within the nation's heart. As Esau forsook his birthright, so has America forsaken its declaration as being "one nation under God."

Chapter 7
Dwelling in the Clefts of the Rock

The next important correlation between the Edomites and the United States is found in verse 3, where it says: "thou that dwellest in the clefts of the rock, whose habitation *is* high; that saith in his heart, Who shall bring me down to the ground?" (KJV) The extension of the Edomites' pride once again is reflected in this statement. As we covered in chapter two, the reasons behind Edom's pride were these: Edom was situated at a high elevation in the rocky reddish sandstone and marble cliffs. This gave the Edomites a significant strategic advantage as would-be attackers would have difficulty reaching them, and certainly could not do so undetected. They also enjoyed the benefits of having natural resources such as rich deposits of copper and iron, and fertile agricultural land in their valleys. Lastly, the main trading routes between Mesopotamia and Egypt passed right through their territory, which gave them another great strategic advantage and supplied a lucrative source of trading revenues from tariffs and taxes. Therefore, the prophetic assessment of Edom—"those dwelling in the clefts of the rock, whose habitation is high"—was not only about being perched high on rocky cliffs, but was a metaphor for its high standard of living.

Once again, we have direct parallels to the United States. With two great oceans on either coast, the United States is strategically situated. Because of our geographic location, great distances of ocean have to be crossed to reach our shores. For example, Japan is over 6,000 miles away, China is over 7,200 miles, North Korea is 6,400 miles, Europe 4,900 miles, Africa 8,900 miles, Russia is over 5,500 miles (not including the closeness of Russia to Alaska), and the Middle East is 7,100 miles away from America. These great distances alone make America very difficult for a foreign military to invade or even attack. There is no chance that an invading army could overrun this nation as Hitler was able to do in Europe. The closest and only attack by a foreign military was the Empire of Japan in World War II. However, the closest they came was Hawaii, which is over 2,300 miles from the mainland.

Like the ancient Edomites, America too, has abundant mineral resources, which include coal, iron ore, bauxite, copper, natural gas, petroleum, mercury, nickel, potash, and silver. Agricultural resources are also abundant. America produces most of the world's corn, meat, cotton, soybeans, tobacco, and wheat. Along with the most powerful overall industrial and military complex in many sectors,

America leads the world. Though America is tenth in the world in per capita income, the nine other nations are not world superpowers and do not have nearly all of the resources and benefits of the United States. America has some of the world's largest, most productive and innovative corporations and businesses that contribute to it having the largest gross national product (GNP) in the world. All of this contributes to America's high standard of living.

Even America's poorest have a better standard of living in comparison to countries like Malawi, because the poor nations in the world do not have enough governmental infrastructure that can provide basic things like clean water and sanitation to their poor. Billions of people around the world do not have access to clean water, a sewage system, or utilities. In America, a homeless person could find money on the street and walk into a grocery store and buy themselves something to eat. In some countries, there are no grocery stores. America has a stable government that is not in danger of being overthrown and has the infrastructure to support an advanced, populous society. We have welfare systems for the poor, and additional resources for the mentally challenged and aged. When comparing America's standard of living to many parts of the world, the statistics are astounding. Eighty percent of the world's population lives on less than $10 a day.[51] Many of these people live in countries that do not have labor laws and are forced to work 16 to 18 hours a day. That being the case, $10 a day would mean working for $0.62 an hour. Even more astounding, a large percentage of the 80 percent live on less than a dollar a day. In those countries, if you are hungry you may easily starve to death on the streets with no assistance from anyone. Here in America, a homeless person can walk into a shelter and get two or three hot meals a day. Many people around the world would kill for the chance to come here and experience the typical benefits of living in America that the average American takes for granted.

When it comes to wealth, America has 515 billionaires, more billionaires than any other country in the world. China is a distant second with 157.[52] America also leads the world in the number of millionaires, which is approximately 4.3 million.[53] America, being a free capitalist society, makes it possible for anyone to strike it rich. There are countless rags to riches stories in the United States that regularly occur, even those who win the lottery. Though the odds of winning the lottery are in the multiplied millions to one, the fact is, in most cases, there is a winner(s) in each drawing. The largest jackpots in the world have been won in America.

All of these factors put together add up to America feeling secure and self-sufficient, particularly since we have no one to answer to and have the power to act unilaterally on the world stage. Therefore, when Americans look around the world from our elevated national platform, we say in our hearts, "Who is able to bring us down to the ground?" What Hitler could rise to bring us down? What Mussolini could bring us down to the ground? What tyrant or terrorist shall bring us down to the ground? What communist or socialist nation could bring us down to the ground?

The following is an excerpt from President Abraham Lincoln's speech, known as the *Lyceum Address*, given in Springfield, Illinois, on January 27, 1838.

> Shall we expect some transatlantic military giant to step the ocean and crush us at a blow? Never! All the armies of Europe, Asia, and Africa combined, with all the treasure of the earth (our own excepted) in their military chest, with a Bonaparte for a commander, could not by force take a drink from the Ohio or make a track on the Blue Ridge in a trial of a thousand years. At what point then is the approach of danger to be expected? I answer. If it ever reach us it must spring up amongst us; it cannot come from abroad. If destruction be our lot we must ourselves be its author and finisher. As a nation of freemen we must live through all time or die by suicide.[54]

In this address, President Lincoln's sagacity is noteworthy, because from his nineteenth-century vantage point, he could see that America did not have to worry about an invader led by some tyrant across the Atlantic Ocean to overthrow her. More importantly, his concern was *"If it ever reach us it must spring up amongst us; it cannot come from abroad. If destruction be our lot we must ourselves be its author and finisher."* Lincoln's assessment of America's demise is close to what is being espoused in this book in this regard: America's problem is not a foreign problem. America's problem is an internal problem that if not corrected threatens to destroy the very foundation of this nation. The Bible warns, "Pride *goes* before destruction, And a haughty spirit before a fall" (Proverbs 16:18, NKJV). As we covered previously, pride precedes destruction because it disregards the first principle, which is, "The fear of the Lord *is* the beginning of wisdom..." (Psalm 111:10, NKJV).

It is God who created the world and laid its foundations. It is God who spread out the oceans and divided the great continents. It is God who placed riches in the earth, the gold and the silver, the copper and the iron, the diamonds and the petroleum. All of the resources come from Him! It is God who raised up human beings, made them in His image, and gave them the charge to be fruitful, multiply, and subdue the earth. It is God that gave man the ability and the power to get wealth, through ideas and inventions inspired by God for men to develop and create. America once knew this. America once acknowledged this! America once reverenced God, in her goings and her comings. But now that America has been blessed, in pride she has turned her back on God, and because of her riches, because of her power, because of influence, because of her strength, she has been puffed up against the very God that has raised her up. Due to all of her beauty, power, and riches, pride has been found in her heart. It shall also be her downfall. Wickedness and calamity shall overtake her, and none shall deliver her. "The pride of her heart has deceived her. Those that dwell in the clefts of the rocks say, who shall bring me down to the ground?" The answer, because of your pride—God.

Chapter 8
Exalt Thyself as the Eagle

As we continue examining similarities between the aspects of Obadiah's prophecy and the United States, this next correlation is quite remarkable. For the purposes of this study, the first seven words of verse 4a in the *King James Version* say it best: "Though thou exalt thyself as the eagle...," and are worthy of an investigation independent of the b-clause of the verse. The word *exalt* comes from the Hebrew word *gābah,*[55] a verb, and a primitive root meaning "*to soar*, i.e., *be lofty*; figurative to be haughty: exalt, be haughty, be (make) high (-er), lift up, mount up, be proud, raise up great height, upward."[56] Therefore, some translations like the *NIV* render *gābah* as "soar," whereas the *NKJV* renders it as "ascend," and the *NASB* renders it "to build high." However, when you consider the figurative definitions such as "to be haughty, lift up, or to be proud," these definitions better capture the intent of the prophet, who was prophesying against Edom's arrogance. A nation can "soar high" and be God-fearing and not be arrogant. However, it wasn't so much the "soaring high" as it was "the arrogance" that the prophet was citing against Edom. For that reason, the rendering of the KJV exalt *thyself* (added by the translators) is preferred by KJV translators as well as this author.

Though this text does not imply that the Edomites had an eagle as their national symbol, the fact that Obadiah, by the Spirit, uses the eagle, cannot be overlooked. Since comparisons between the ancient Edomites and the United States are being made, at the very least the semantics are noteworthy, because America's symbol is the eagle. Alone, coincidental, but compelling when considered with the body of other correlations being made in this book.

When a nation chooses a national symbol, much thought goes into that process. Each nation chooses a symbol that best portrays the essence, character, and philosophy of its people. There is no room for incongruence. A swift and aggressive nation would not choose a snail as a national symbol. Therefore, the question concerning how America chose the eagle to be its national symbol is an important part of this study.

Using animals as national symbols goes back thousands of years because people related to animals based upon their unique instinctive and distinctive characteristics. Using animals to symbolize the character of a nation can also be found in the Bible. For example, in the book of Daniel, God characterizes Babylon as a lion, Medo-Persia as a bear, Greece as a leopard and Rome as a monstrous beast. Rome's depiction was not comparable to any of the known wild animals, but was given more of a mystical description as a "beast" having iron teeth and ten horns. These symbolic identifications are not arbitrary but have prophetic significance. The *Tyndale Commentary* observes the following:

> In eagerness to identify the beasts, it is important not to miss the emotional reactions these fierce symbols arouse. 'Signals and signs operate almost entirely at the rational and conscious level to convey compressed meanings which are known to the participants. Symbols proliferate meanings and associations in the unconscious mind and feelings.'[57]

As stated above, "symbols convey compressed meanings which are known to the participants." Therefore, when a nation chooses a symbol, an animal in particular, it is a reflection of that nation's philosophy and potential, in both its present and future survival and conquests. Those aspirations are then propagated by its government onto its citizenry and form the basis for a collective consciousness which is actualized through allegiance and a sense of national pride and support.

When it comes to Obadiah's observation of Edom as an eagle, again, I am not suggesting that Obadiah had an apocalyptic vision and saw the United States per se. However, I am drawing these conclusions using Edom as a template for the United States. Throughout this book, we have aligned several significant correlations between the two. The fact that God used the eagle analogy to prophesy against the Edomites is just another similarity that helps paint a prophetic portrait for the future of the United States.

Throughout history, there have been many nations that have used the eagle on their coat of arms, national flag, and other official usages. This speaks to the universality of the eagle's superiority among other fowls. According to the *American Heritage Dictionary*, an *eagle* is "any of various large diurnal birds of prey of the family *Accipitridae*, including members of the genera *Aquila* and *Haliaeetus*, characterized by a powerful hooked bill, keen vision, long broad wings, and strong, soaring flight."[58]

Eagles belong to several groups of genera that are not necessarily closely related to each other. The majority of the sixty species of eagles are from Eurasia and Africa. Only fourteen species can be found outside of these two continents, two of which are found in North America. The two species found in America are the golden eagle and the bald eagle, the latter being the symbol of the United States.

Eagles typically build their nests, in tall trees or high up on cliffs. Once eagles are hatched, their predator instincts trigger almost immediately. Since many species lay two eggs, the older and usually larger chick frequently kills the younger sibling once it has hatched. The dominant chick tends to be a female, as females are bigger than the males. Interestingly, the parents take no action to stop the fratricide.

Due to the size and supremacy of many eagle species, they are ranked at the top of the avian food chain and as such are considered apex predators. Eagles kill with their feet and talons (long razor-sharp claws). This is remarkable. Not only are eagles impressively large raptors with a seven-foot wingspan, but their gripping power is as much as ten times stronger than an adult man, producing 400 psi of pressure.

The American National Symbol

The bald eagle's role as a national symbol is connected to its use on the Great Seal of the United States in 1782. Shortly after the signing of the Declaration of Independence on July 4, 1776, the Continental Congress gave Benjamin Franklin, Thomas Jefferson, and John Adams the job of designing an official seal for the new nation. However, they could not come up with a design that won Congress' approval. After their inability to submit a suitable design, the task was given to two subsequent committees. In mid-June 1782, the work of all three committees was handed over to Charles Thomson, the secretary of Congress. Thomson chose what he thought were the best elements of the various designs and made the eagle, which had been introduced by Pennsylvania lawyer and artist William Barton in a design submitted by the third committee, more prominent.

Thomson also recommended that the small, white eagle used in Barton's design be replaced with an American bald eagle. This was the design that Congress adopted on June 20, 1782. Ironically, in 1784, Benjamin Franklin wrote in a letter to his daughter labeling the bald eagle "a bird of bad moral character," therefore not a favorable choice. Additionally, there is no historical evidence that Benjamin Franklin actually lobbied for the national bird being a turkey. This claim seems to be folklore without any historical merit.

The new design portraying the eagle went on to appear on official documents, currency, flags, public buildings, and other government-related items, thereby making the bald eagle an American icon.[59] President John F. Kennedy once wrote to Charles Callison of the National Audubon Society on July 18, 1961: "The founding fathers made an appropriate choice when they selected the bald eagle as the emblem of the nation. The fierce beauty and proud independence of this great bird aptly symbolizes the strength and freedom of America."[60]

Eagles and the Native American Culture

Now that we have some historical perspective on how the eagle became the national bird and a prominent feature on the United States' Great Seal, another historic reality that cannot be overlooked is the role eagles played in the day-to-day and customary lives of the Native Americans (Indigenous People). Long before Europeans landed on the shores of America, the Indigenous People expressed a great admiration and respect for the great eagles of America.

Here is a brief excerpt revealing the role that eagles played in the lives of Native American tribes all over what is now known as the United States.

> Both Bald and Golden Eagles (and their feathers) are highly revered and considered sacred within Native Americans' traditions, culture and religion. They are honored with great care and shown the deepest respect. They represent honesty, truth, majesty, strength, courage, wisdom, power and freedom. As they roam the sky, they are believed to have a special connection to God.
>
> According to traditional American Indian beliefs, the Creator made all the birds of the sky when the World was new. Of all the birds, the Creator chose the Eagle to be the leader... the Master of the Sky.
>
> The Eagle flies higher and sees better than any other bird. Therefore, its perspective is different from other creations that are held close to the Earth, and it is closer to the Creator. The Creator also has a different perspective of what occurs below in this world of physical things in which humankind resides. The Eagle spends more time in the higher element of Father Sky than other birds...."[61]
>
> — *Indigenous Spiritual Leaders of the Americas*

From this we can conclude that America's choice of the eagle was not only the appropriate symbol to use, but it was also providential in that Native Americans had the same high regard for the eagle hundreds, perhaps thousands of years prior to European colonization.

CHAPTER 9
A NEST AMONG THE STARS

One of the most fascinating aspects about the Bible that sets it above all other sacred writings is prophecy. The accuracy of prophetic fulfillment is astounding, as we will see in the next aspect of Obadiah's prophecy. In the following phrase in verse 4, a remarkable likeness to the United States is found once again. The phrase reads: "though thou set thy nest among the stars, thence will I bring thee down, saith the LORD." In its grammatical-historical context, this passage is a response to the Edomites' assertion found in verse 3, taking the position of pride, they said in their hearts "who shall bring me down to the ground," meaning bringing them down from their high position as a nation. Figuratively, this was emphasized by saying that they have a "nest among the stars."

Opening verse 3 is the indictment against the Edomites that says "the pride of thy heart has deceived you." This is quite foreboding. Clearly, the Edomites were doomed to destruction, being victims of their own arrogance. Through pride, they figuratively lived "up high," but simultaneously they literally lived up high because of their high standard of living spurred by a strong economy. They also lived high up because they were situated in the clefts of the rocks, perched at a high elevation, which led them to mistakenly believe that they were untouchable. In their skewed reasoning, they boasted "who shall bring me down to the ground?" However, though they may have been too high to reach by would-be enemies, they were not out of reach for an almighty, omnipresent God.

The combination of figurative and literal interpretation of this prophecy must not be overlooked, as this certainly applies when aligning this prophecy with the United States. What we have today that Obadiah did not have is three thousand years of hindsight. Now we have come to the age of technological advancement that could render a literal meaning to a prophetic statement that in millennia past could only have been interpreted figuratively. For decades, it is a fact that the United States has led the world in space exploration and now actually has nests among the stars.

On Christmas Eve 1968, the crew of Apollo 8, Commander Frank Borman, Command Module Pilot James Lovell, and Lunar Module Pilot William Anders, were the first people to travel beyond low-Earth orbit, and were the first humans to see Earth as a whole planet. This was a revolutionary first step on a long journey in outer space exploration. Indeed, these were the first men who directly saw the far side of the moon, and from a lunar perspective, the first people to witness an Earth-rise.

In commemoration of this monumental moment in history, each member of the Apollo 8 read from Genesis, chapter one, in succession beginning with Bill Anders, then Jim Lovell, and closing with Frank Borman's quotation from the Scriptures as follows:

> "And God said, Let the waters under the heavens be gathered together unto one place, and let the dry land appear: and it was so. And God called the dry land Earth; and the gathering together of the waters called he seas: and God saw that it was good."

Borman then closed by saying, "And from the crew of Apollo 8, we close with good night, good luck, a Merry Christmas, and God bless all of you—all of you on the good Earth."

During the 1960s, for most Americans, hearing the Bible being read or God being referenced was not that unusual or offensive, even though there were some who protested the astronauts reading the Bible on a government spacecraft. The majority of Americans had no problem with reading the Bible or acknowledging God, especially on Christmas Eve. The Apollo crew did not have to worry about being politically incorrect, because back then, it was acceptable to invoke and acknowledge God on historical occasions. However, today, the God that the Apollo crew acknowledged as the Creator of all things in heaven and on earth, who gave man the intelligence and ingenuity to go into outer space, could not read the Bible or even acknowledge God. In today's social and political climate, this would have been a source of outrage.

The Russians were four years ahead of the United States in space; their first flight was 1957. However, the United States vowed to be the winners of the "space race." For the following decades NASA put billions of dollars into a very active space exploration program. On May 25, 1961, President John F. Kennedy announced before Congress the dramatic and ambitious goal of sending an American to the moon before the end of the decade. As many historians observe, Kennedy's announcement was the result of pressure to have the United States "catch up to and overtake" the Soviet Union in the "space race." On May 25, 1961, President Kennedy before Congress stated:

> "We choose to go to the moon in this decade and do the other things, not because they are easy, but because they are hard, because that goal will serve to organize and measure the best of our energies and skills, because that challenge is one that we are willing to accept, one we are unwilling to postpone, and one which we intend to win."

Going farther into outer space became a mission and calling for the United States that ignited an explosion in space technology and exploration that continues to this day.

"The Eagle has Landed"

Eight years had passed since Kennedy's prediction of landing men on the moon. Finally, it was about to happen. The Apollo 11 mission would be the first time that human beings stepped foot on an extraterrestrial surface. With bated breath millions of people all over the world were glued to their radios and televisions waiting to hear or see if Apollo 11 had made it onto the lunar surface. On July 20, 1969 at 20:18, the lunar module, appropriately named "the Eagle" after the bald eagle of the Great Seal of the United States, touched down on the moon. It was at this point that Neil Armstrong radioed back to earth, "The Eagle has landed." The next day, he stepped out of the lunar module and onto the moon's surface and made his historic proclamation: "One small step for a man, one giant leap for mankind."

While these national heroes were still on the lunar surface, President Richard Nixon made these comments to Neil Armstrong and Buzz Aldrin during a phone call to them in outer space.

> Neil and Buzz. . . Because of what you have done, the heavens have become a part of man's world. As you talk to us from the Sea of Tranquility, it inspires us to redouble our efforts to bring peace and tranquility to Earth.

After this triumphant event, America continued to send men to the moon, although the idea of having a base on the moon was scrapped. America's manned space program continued for several years, with the launch of Skylab, America's first space station, followed by several space shuttle missions. After the space shuttle missions, America stopped manned flights, opting for more unmanned exploration, while private industries' forays into space exploration became dominant. America also launched many space explorations, sending probes to Mars, Jupiter, Neptune, Uranus, and Pluto and beyond.

In the Bible, there is at least one passage of Scripture whose fulfillment requires technology in outer space. For example, a passage in the book of Revelation intimates the necessity of outer space technology when speaking of the circumstances surrounding the enigmatic "Two Witnesses" of Revelation, chapter 11. Though time does not permit me to conduct a detailed analysis of the Scriptures dealing with the Two Witnesses, there is an interesting passage that presumes human involvement in outer space.

After the Two Witnesses are killed, the Bible gives us some details that a pre-scientific-age prophet of the first century could not have possibly understood. The passage reads:

> For three and a half days some from every people, tribe, language and nation will gaze on their bodies and refuse them burial. The inhabitants of the earth will gloat over them and will celebrate by sending each other gifts, because these two prophets had tormented those who live on the earth. But after the three and a half days the breath of life from God entered them, and they stood on their feet, and terror struck those who saw them. Then they heard a loud voice from heaven saying to them, "Come up here." And they went up to heaven in a cloud, while their enemies looked on.
>
> Revelation 11:9-12, NIV 2011

Tacit inside this passage is information about a technologically advanced world that could not have been fulfilled prior to the latter half of the twentieth century. Verse 9 states explicitly, "For three and a half days some from every people, tribe, language and nation will gaze on their bodies." Here is what John MacArthur says concerning this prophetic account:

> The use of the all-inclusive phrase peoples and tribes and tongues and nations (cf. 5:9; 7:9; 10:11) indicates that people around the world will look at the dead bodies of the two witnesses (on satellite television or some other form of visual media).[62]

We clearly understand today what the apostle John could not have possibly known about technology belonging to the twentieth and twenty-first centuries. Nevertheless, he accurately states the truth about people all over the world being able to see the Two Witnesses' dead bodies lying in the streets. Today we understand this to be possible through satellite communication that allows television signals to be transmitted live around the world in real-time.

Considering everything covered here about America's role in outer space, you cannot simply walk away seeing Obadiah's prophecy as mere coincidence. It is not about America being first in space or having the most missions launched. What is important is America's utilization of space in the normal course of life. Everything from television broadcasts, GPS systems, smartphone functions, telephone service, cloud services, satellite radio, top-secret satellites, and military drones are all outgrowths of America's expansive space program.

As we have discovered, the eagle flies high and builds its nest higher than most birds. It has keen eyesight that allows it to see small prey on the ground from high elevations. So scientifically, has the American eagle through space platforms like the Hubble space telescope peered deeply into outer space. Images from galaxies as far away as 13 billion light years have come into clear view from an eagle's nest set high among the stars.

Chapter 10
As You Have Done, it Shall be Done to You

In this chapter, we shall examine the final correlation between ancient Edom and America, which is taken from verse 15. Our text reads:

> The day of the Lord is near for all nations. As you have done, it will be done to you; your deeds will return upon your own head.

In chapter two, we conducted a cursory review of the eschatological term called the "Day of the Lord," which is synonymous with the "wrath of God" being poured out on the world and culminating with the Lord returning in His glory. The dramatic aspects of the Day of the Lord referenced in many books of the Bible in both the Old and New Testaments are informative. However, it is more graphically depicted in the book of Revelation, and is characterized by Jesus "as being a day of trouble not since the beginning of time, nor will ever be." In Romans 1, the apostle Paul sets the context for the wrath of God when he writes:

> The wrath of God is being revealed from heaven against all the godlessness and wickedness of people, who suppress the truth by their wickedness, since what may be known about God is plain to them, because God has made it plain to them. For since the creation of the world God's invisible qualities—his eternal power and divine nature—have been clearly seen, being understood from what has been made, so that people are without excuse.
>
> Verses18-20, NIV 2011

In these two verses, Paul introduces us to the basis for why God's wrath will ultimately be revealed (unveiled) against the wickedness of a world gone wild. The problem is, the world is blind to the truth of God and does not see itself as wicked. It sees itself as liberated, free to express its desires and values without being judged by man or by God. The important thing to understand is, the kind of world we have is the kind of world you get when nations continuously reject God. In essence, we have exchanged God's truth for a lie. This is the same thing that Adam and Eve did in the garden when tempted by the devil. Satan's lie became their truth, which opened their eyes to darkness. Darkness then became their light.

Therefore, in a secular, anti-God society, *relativism* defines morality. Relativism is a segment of philosophy that teaches the theory that conceptions of truth and moral values are not absolute but are relative to the persons or groups holding them. In that kind of world, everybody does what is right in their own eyes.

Without moral absolutes setting the parameters of what

is and what is not acceptable, societies fall prey to the debased and wicked desires of depraved human hearts. After going so far in that direction, eventually their wickedness, as Genesis 18 says about Sodom, reaches God. In Genesis 18, we read:

> And the LORD said, "Because the outcry against Sodom and Gomorrah is great, and because their sin is very grave, I will go down now and see whether they have done altogether according to the outcry against it that has come to Me; and if not, I will know."
>
> Verses 20-21, NKJV

This is what has happened to America. America has continuously rejected the righteousness of God, and now her sins cry out against her. As Esau, America in a sense has sold her birthright for a big bowl of green capitalist soup, and has forsaken her God-given blessing. Therefore, the good that she has done will not save her, but her wickedness will be the basis for her reward. As Obadiah 1:15 says, as America has done to others (her own people and other nations), it shall be done to her.

Think about the ramifications of America getting back what she has dished out. It is too terrifying to contemplate! The principle is called *sowing and reaping*. You reap what you sow, but you reap much more than you sow. If you sow one kernel of corn, you reap a corn stalk with many ears of corn bearing thousands of kernels of corn. If you sow to the wind, you reap the whirlwind (see Hosea 8:7). A more contemporary definition of a whirlwind would be a hurricane. Or, what we in the United States are equally familiar with, the tornado, the most violent concentrated whirlwind on earth.

The Average American Doesn't Have a Clue

Though there are countries that edge out America in a few categories, across the board America has the best the world has to offer. Recently, I was out celebrating my birthday with my wife. While we were having dinner, there was a couple sitting at the table next to us celebrating their 35th anniversary. After striking up a conversation, they spoke about having visited Rome. His comment was, "Americans have no idea how good we have it here." He went on to say that he was surprised how dirty Rome actually is. "We have higher standards here in the States," he insisted. My thoughts after he made that statement were, he's right that Americans don't have a clue about the standards abroad, or about the standards right here in America. Obviously, he had not walked the streets of America's poorest communities, where he would have seen the filthy conditions and the destitute living right here.

Like the Edomites, we Americans see the world through the lens of our privilege. We expect things to be elsewhere as they are here. When they are not, we tend to have a critical attitude. We often carry an air that we are entitled to other nations' respect because we are the world's great superpower, the most influential nation in the world. However, there is a big difference between being *respected* and being *liked*. I respect a pit bull, but I don't like them.

In general, Americans don't think about themselves in a negative light. That within itself is typical of most nations and cultures. The principal problem concerning America is that we have our hands in so many geopolitical cookie jars. That is what makes America such a big target for those hurling criticism our way. While we see ourselves as the great helper of the world, other nations see us as a big meddler who can't mind its own business. Nevertheless, we Americans do not see ourselves that way.

Much of what we think about is fed to us through the various forms of media. The average American watches five hours of television per day.[63] Over a lifespan of seventy years, that is approximately fourteen years spent in front of a television. Smartphones and computers add even more time. Even though there are still some who get information from printed materials such as newspapers and magazines, that's quickly shifting to electronic media, which is predominately entertainment- based. Even the evening news is entertainment. Americans are probably among the most entertained people in the world. We love our evening game shows, our weekly serials, our sports events, our award shows, our concerts, our tabloid news, and our breaking world news. Controversy is another big media draw that has many Americans addicted; the more outrageous, the better. But has anyone ever stopped to think about why we are inundated with so much information? Who is behind all of this massive media messaging and information? And whose agenda are we actually pursuing?

May I submit that there are two Americas. The first we know through what we are told and what we see through our day-to-day experiences in society or through the various forms of media. The second is a secret America—the one that enforces the agenda of the powerful elites, acts covertly, and pursues government interests at the expense of others around the world. These "others" are people whom we will never see, know, or even care about. This is important, because as Obadiah prophesied, "As you have done, it will be done to you; your deeds will return upon your own head."

When we purchase that new clothing item, or the pair of gym shoes, or purchase the latest cellphone, we don't think about, care about, or care to know about the conditions and the blood, sweat and tears, or the toll of human suffering and oppression that make these products available in our stores. We don't concern ourselves with the details; we just want to look good wearing the clothes. From the retailer's point of view, if there is money to be made, do it, sell it, and don't worry about how it was made. Unfortunately, this is how capitalism works. Capitalism by nature cares about profits, not people.

This secret America works behind the scenes, particularly in other countries. This is what the CIA does. The CIA is prohibited from operating inside the United States and is tasked with securing and maintaining our national interests around the world. Even if it means killing, stealing, and overthrowing governments through *coup d'états*, or by backing revolutions with money and munitions to put puppet regimes that will do America's bidding. Around the world, America plays many under-the-table games, many of which are despicable. Some of the things our country is responsible for around the world would astound and appall the average American. However, the CIA is not behind everything—we also have corporations, international banks, the military, and even powerful religious entities that operate covertly beyond our borders. This is the stuff that never makes it to our evening news or shows up as headlines in our newspapers. What the CIA does overseas is highly classified, and it is illegal to "out" a CIA operative. You can go to federal prison for doing so.

However, overseas is not where all of America's dirty laundry is—we have plenty hiding in our own closets. All the classism, racism, sexism, inequalities faced by the minorities, the political, corporate and religious corruption, all of the violence—America is one of the most violent democracies on earth. In a nation with all of this wealth, why are there so many people who are impoverished? In a country with so much freedom, why do we incarcerate more people than any other country in the world, the vast majority of those being black and other minorities? In a country with the best legal system in the world, why is there so much injustice? In a country with the best educational system, why are there so many undereducated students who attend underperforming schools? In a country with so much opportunity to get ahead, why are so many people left behind and denied opportunities and not given a fair chance? These are compelling reasons why, if America is to reap the same things she has done to others, we are in serious trouble.

One might ask, what about all of the good that this nation has done? The response would be, "What about it?" To whom much is given, much is required—that's the cost, not the dividend. We have the *responsibility* to be generous because we were given so much. God does not owe us anything—we owe Him! How we help others is how we show our gratitude to Him, beginning here at home. Don't tell me about how to fix the leaks in my roof when there is a gaping hole in yours.

America has invaded and occupied other nations, almost wiped out an indigenous population, we're the only ones to drop atom bombs on another civilization, set sanctions on nations that have starved and deprived other people, enforced legalized slavery for over 250 years, encouraged and backed the overthrow of other governments, and the list goes on and on.

Of course, most of these things can be justified under the banner of securing our national interests. However, that by itself is problematic, particularly when it's at the expense of other people and nations around the world. There are many who would tout that we must maintain America's foreign and national interests around the world to keep a high standard of living at home. Nevertheless, no matter how we seek to justify our actions, we cannot skirt the issue. The Bible says, "As you have done, it will be done to you; your deeds will return upon your own head." This is a rule or standard for judgment where the justifications for the actions will not give us a pass. America will reap for what it has done to others, and the reasons for doing them will not be mitigating.

A Legacy of Violence

"Living by the Sword"

As I add the closing remarks to this book, another mass shooting has occurred in America at Umpqua Community College in Umpqua, Oregon. Ten people, including the gunman, were killed, and several others were wounded. Apparently, the gunman asked the victims if they were Christians. If they responded yes, they were shot in the head. If they didn't respond, they were shot in the leg. Making a passionate statement from the White House, President Obama said, "This is happening too regularly." He's right. In the last 100 years there have been 156 mass shootings in America, where four or more people have been killed in public with guns within 24 hours, excluding crimes such as robberies, gang wars, or drug trafficking, etc.[64] According to *Newsweek*, this latest shooting makes the 45th school shooting in America in 2015 alone.[65]

Obviously, when tragedies of this proportion occur, everyone asks, "What in the world is happening to this nation?" The answer can be traced back to Esau.

As the Genesis account states, after Jacob stole Esau's blessing, Esau begged his father Isaac to bless him anyway. However, the leftover blessing he received is found in the following passage:

> His father Isaac answered him, "Your dwelling will be away from the earth's richness, away from the dew of heaven above. You will live by the sword…."
>
> Genesis 27:39-40, NIV 2011

To live "by the sword" was an Old Testament idiom meaning to live by force or violence. Going back to Esau, he was the man of the field, the hunter, the predator. He was good with a weapon; his ability to use his sword and his bow and arrow is what he trusted in the most. His character was to take by force. Unlike his brother Jacob, who the Bible says was domesticated, "living in the tents," Esau had a wilder unruly character who would rather trust in his ability to fight rather than trust in God. In the same spirit as their progenitor, the Edomites were a warlike people that fought numerous battles against Israel (2 Kings 8:20, 2 Chronicles 21:8-10, 28:16-17).

In the spirit of Esau, America too has a legacy of violence. Though America has contributed greatly to world peace, make no mistake about it, it's because it had the military power to enforce peace. This is what President Theodore Roosevelt meant when he said "speak softly, but carry a big stick." This is the idea of negotiating peacefully, while simultaneously threatening with a "big stick," or the military. Therefore, America's peace comes by her ability and readiness to make war. This is why on America's Great Seal, the eagle is holding in its right talon an olive branch, symbolizing peace, while in the left talon, it clutches thirteen arrows symbolizing war. The meaning of the olive branch and the thirteen arrows is "the power of peace and war."[66]

According to documentary filmmaker, writer and controversial radio talk show host Alex Jones, since 1776, the year of America's independence, the United States has been involved in some type of war, conflict, covert action, police or military campaign, etc., either at home or somewhere else in the world. As of 2015, it has been 239 years since our independence, 223 of those years in which our nation has been involved in some type of conflict. Astoundingly, that is about 93% of the time since we have been an independent nation that we have been at war.[67]

War and conflict are in America's DNA. This is why the right to bear arms is so dear to Americans. The Second Amendment states: "A well-regulated militia being necessary to the security of a free state, the right of the people to keep and bear arms shall not be infringed." The right to bear arms is a very important right. I believe that a person should have the right to own a gun. However, the natural outgrowth of that right is gun violence. In America today, there are approximately 300 million guns. That is almost one gun for each person in this country. However, those firearms are not spread out evenly amongst all adults. For example, in Alaska 62 percent of adults own a gun, whereas, in Delaware, only 5 percent own a gun.[68] Contrary to popular belief, thugs, drug dealers, and gang bangers in inner-city urban areas do not possess the majority of the guns. "The most likely demographic group to own a gun, according to the study, are white males over 55 who have finished high school and are, or have been, married. Unsurprisingly, gun owners are more than twice as likely as non-owners to be part of a "social gun culture" in which family and friends often own guns and look down on non-gun owners."[69]

National organizations like the National Rifle Association (NRA), one of the most powerful lobbying groups in America, tenaciously advocate for the right of American citizens to bear arms. The Second Amendment right to bear arms is held in very high esteem and to many is a "sacred" right. However, the natural outgrowth of easy availability of firearms makes "America the Beautiful" dangerous and massacres like Columbine, Sandy Hook, Aurora, Colorado, Virginia Tech, the Emanuel AME Church in Charleston, South Carolina, and countless others possible. Unfortunately, living by the sword will cause many to die by the sword. Many of our blockbuster films are violent, many of our weekly television shows are violent, our massive video game industry produces numerous violently graphic video games, and more and more sports have become increasingly violent. We distribute all of this virtual violence, then wonder why our nation is becoming so violent. America sells more guns to its citizens than any nation on earth. Our government exports more armament, weapons, and munitions than any country on earth. The death toll from American-made weapons around the world is incalculable.

However, the most violent place in America is not on our urban streets, but is in the mother's womb. According to LifeNews.com, since *Roe vs. Wade*, over fifty-seven million abortions have occurred in the United States.

So, the answer to "Why is America so violent?" It's simple: "As you have done to others, it shall be done unto you."

Chapter 11
Turn this Nation Around!
The Hope for America

After reading all of what has been presented in this book, the obvious question would be, "Is there hope for America?" The answer to that question cannot be found on Capitol Hill or the courtrooms of our justice system. Nor can it be found in the legislative or executive branches of government. The answer cannot be found by the Federal Reserve Bank or in the great financial institutions of this nation. The answer will not be found by philosophers, sociologists, or educators. The answer will not be found by the military or by technological advances. If America continues on its current course, no manmade institutions, systems, or processes will be able to stop God's wrath from being poured out on this nation. As I once heard Dr. Tony Evans say in one of his inspiring sermons, "If God is your problem, then only God is your solution." If America is going to escape judgment and become a model of a righteous nation, then we must turn back to God to turn this nation around!

America, like other nations throughout history, was

never perfect. From the very beginning, America struggled with its "original sin"—chattel slavery and the slaughter of Native Americans. However, America did have many good qualities. This used to be a country that acknowledged the grace of God and that by His providence was destined to be great. Granted, the framers of our Constitution were not clergymen, and our governmental structure was never theocratic, but the framers had a reverence for God who is the Creator and the Sustainer of all things.

There was a time when our government embraced the idea that "God shed His grace on America." At one time, we were proud of our national motto "In God We Trust." As students throughout the United States recited *The Pledge of Allegiance* each morning at the beginning of class, we did not protest against the fact that we were, "one nation under God."

Interestingly, "one nation under God" was not originally in the *Pledge of Allegiance*. In 1954, it was added at President Dwight D. Eisenhower's urging, with Congress legislating in favor of "one nation under God" being added to the Pledge.[70] Though this symbolic action was a response to atheistic communism, the fact that Eisenhower chose this insertion shows the importance the President and members of Congress placed on reverencing the God of Glory. However, are we that nation that would do the same thing today? Or have we sided with the forces of "freedom from religion," exalting human rights above God's moral law?

In the book of Jeremiah, chapter 2, we find God's appeal to Jerusalem:

> The word of the Lord came to me: "Go and proclaim in the hearing of Jerusalem: "This is what the Lord says: "'I remember the devotion of your youth, how as a bride you loved me and followed me through the wilderness, through a land not sown. Israel was holy to the Lord, the first fruits of his harvest; all who devoured her were held guilty, and disaster overtook them,'" declares the Lord.
>
> Verses1-3, NIV 2011

This passage is full of God's passion for His chosen people. He pleads with Jerusalem: remember how you used to be towards Me. You were close to Me, you trusted in Me, and all those who came up against you, I fought against and brought disasters upon them. Here God is pleading with His people, "Come back to me! Make it as it used to be, when you reverenced and respected Me. You honored Me and gave Me the glory for all the blessings that I bestowed upon you." It is if God is saying today:

> Come back to Me, America, I love you. I raised you up. I called you here, even though you were orphans in your own homeland, I brought you to these fertile shores and reserved the best for you. I handpicked the cultures and ethnicities that came here. I gave you those amber waves of grain; I raised up those purple mountains' majesty, and I spread out those fruited plains. I gave you the beautiful land that stretches from sea to shining sea. You were once proud to sing, "God Bless America." I made America great so that the world through you would learn of Me. I made America great so that the Church could flourish and evangelize the world. So that you would be a nation,

> that is set high upon a hill, above the others, for all the world to see that the blessing of the Lord makes a nation rich without sorrow. I made you great to be an example to the world, that serving God blesses a nation and that walking in righteousness exalts a nation. Before it is too late, America, come back to Me, or you shall be an example of another type with this tragic epitaph: "America, the nation that forgot God, and is now no more."

The City of Nineveh

There is a biblical precedence for God turning His wrath on a people upon whom He had pronounced judgment. This account is found in the book of Jonah, concerning the judgment of the city of Nineveh. We all know the story. God sent Jonah to Nineveh (after Jonah's brief detour) to warn the Ninevites that God was going to overthrow this city in forty days. The Bible tells us that Jonah preached on the streets of this sprawling metropolis, which was a three-day journey. In what might have surprised Jonah, the Bible says: "The Ninevites believed God. A fast was proclaimed, and all of them, from the greatest to the least, put on sackcloth" (Jonah 3:5, NIV 2011). The key words here are, "The Ninevites believed God." In other words, their hearts were pricked and convicted. Like a hammer, God's message crushed their stony hearts and they repented. However, it wasn't just the citizenry that repented, it was the king and the nobles (governmental officials). Here is what's said concerning the king:

> When Jonah's warning reached the king of Nineveh, he rose from his throne, took off his royal robes, covered

> himself with sackcloth and sat down in the dust. This is the proclamation he issued in Nineveh: "By the decree of the king and his nobles: Do not let people or animals, herds or flocks, taste anything; do not let them eat or drink. But let people and animals be covered with sackcloth. Let everyone call urgently on God. Let them give up their evil ways and their violence. Who knows? God may yet relent and with compassion turn from his fierce anger so that we will not perish."
>
> Jonah 3:6-9, NIV 2011

This an example of true national repentance, because it occurred from the top down. The king humbled himself, took off his royal garments, and covered himself in sackcloth and ashes. It was necessary for the king to be an example and actually repent himself. He wasn't prideful and didn't leave that for only the people of Nineveh to do. This too, must occur in America, from the White House to Capitol Hill, to the governors' mansions, to the city halls: everyone must repent. The king said, "Let them give up their evil ways and their violence." Evil ways and wickedness go hand in hand with violence. The more wicked a society is, the more violent it becomes. The amount of violence occurring is a principal indicator of the moral state of that society. Therefore, the Scriptures teach, "When the godly are in authority, the people rejoice. But when the wicked are in power, they groan" (Proverbs 29:2, NLT).

Nineveh's repentance was effective. Jonah 3:10 states, "When God saw what they did and how they turned from their evil ways, he relented and did not bring on them the destruction he had threatened." Nineveh was the benefactor of a conditional prophecy. They met the condition to repent; therefore, the prophecy of destruction was delayed. However, judgment was imminent, because about a century later, after they fell back into national sin, they indeed were destroyed.

In his commentary, Matthew Henry observes:

> About a hundred years before, at Jonah's preaching, the Ninevites repented, and were spared, yet, soon after, they became worse than ever. Nineveh knows not that God who contends with her, but is told what a God he is. It is good for all to mix faith with what is here said concerning Him, which speaks great terror to the wicked, and comfort to believers. Let each take his portion from it: let sinners read it and tremble; and let saints read it and triumph. The anger of the Lord is contrasted with his goodness to his people.[71]

The question that remains is, can America be saved? The answer is, if she continues on her present path—no. If we turn this nation around, perhaps the Lord will be gracious and delay judgment as He did with the Ninevites. Remember, Obadiah's prophecy had an eschatological (end-times) piece to it, about the Day of the Lord, where all the nations would be paid back for all of what they had done to others (see Obadiah 1:15). However, this brings up another issue that requires addressing. American Christians tend to see Christianity as a whole through the lens of an American experience. However, Christendom is not American, and America is not the whole of Christendom. We don't get to say when God is coming back for His

Church, as if He needs to hurry to come deliver American Christians out of their troubles. The Lord will not come back until the fullness of the Gentiles is reached (Romans 11:25). There are people whom God has already foreknown and predestined who are not even born yet. There are people here in America and around the world that are not saved yet, whom God is going to save. We don't know who these people are, but God does.

Ask yourself, did not the Lord wait on you? Did not the Lord wait on your family members? God delays His coming because He knows who all the redeemed are and none of them will be lost. He delays His coming because He has more souls to save. So brothers and sisters of the Church of Jesus Christ, start repenting and calling on the name of the Lord, because we are going to be used to gather the greatest harvest of souls that the world has ever known! As America grows increasingly debased, there will be more persecution of Christians. It's not a matter of if, it is a matter of when. There is a lot the Church during the last days is going to go through. I believe that just as the Church started during the first century, it will be under similar conditions when the Rapture occurs.

My People Who are Called by My Name

One may ask, What if America refuses to repent? What happens then? Should our deliverance as a nation be contingent upon the wicked repenting? For the answer to that question, once again, we must turn to the pages of Scripture. In 2 Chronicles, chapter 7, here is what the Lord has to say:

> When I shut up the heavens so that there is no rain, or command locusts to devour the land or send a plague among my people, if my people, who are called by my name, will humble themselves and pray and seek my face and turn from their wicked ways, then I will hear from heaven, and I will forgive their sin and will heal their land. Now my eyes will be open and my ears attentive to the prayers offered in this place.
>
> Verses 13-15, NIV 2011

Of these three verses, verse 14—"if my people who are called by my name…"—is probably one of the best-known Scriptures in the Old Testament. The *Tyndale Commentary* observes:

> Chapter 7 is not only central to the message of Chronicles, but it is also one of the most important chapters in the Old Testament. It offers hope to any who call on the name of the Lord, even if they have incurred God's wrath, because God's desire is for full reconciliation.[72]

This commentary has touched upon the importance of God's desire is for reconciliation, not wrath. Like a loving Father, He'd much rather be loving and gracious, rather than angry and chastening. However, I would like to expand on this great passage a bit more to emphasize what the Chronicler has emphasized. He reveals a qualifier when he says "if *my* people who are called by *my* name…." The personal pronoun "my" makes all the difference in the world. As we examined concerning the Ninevites, these were not God's people, in the sense of being in a covenantal relationship with God. These were pagan, heathen, and idol-worshipping Gentiles. There were no Abrahamic promises, Mosaic Law, or a Davidic covenant in which to appeal. They had nothing between them and God. These were wicked people, the whole lot of them.

Like Sodom and Gomorrah centuries before them, Nineveh's sins too, had reached up to God. However, for His own providential reasons, He chose to show the Ninevites mercy. When Jonah seemed to take issue with that, God's response was, "And should I not have concern for the great city of Nineveh, in which there are more than a hundred and twenty thousand people who cannot tell their right hand from their left…?" (Jonah 4:11, NIV 2011) These people repented, and Jonah knew that God would be gracious and forgiving towards them, which, in Jonah's mind, they did not deserve. But in the case where the wicked won't repent, what hope could that nation possibly have? The answer is that God will hear the voice of His people, because they bear His name. For our sake, those who bear the name of Jesus, He can delay judgment on America.

Second Chronicles 7:14 gives us the steps for Christians to spur national repentance. The first one is humility. Humility is the antidote for pride and must be the basis on which we approach Almighty God. God told Moses, "Take off your shoes, you are standing on holy ground." It was as if God was saying, "Before you approach me, humble yourself." God is not concerned about your title, your degree, your position, your money, or your status. God is not a respecter of persons. However, what He does respect is a broken heart and a contrite spirit. In order to be healed by God, we need to be humbled before God.

The second step is prayer. In the book of James, the Bible says, "...The effectual fervent prayer of a righteous man availeth much (James 5:16, KJV). In Revelation 8, we find a glorious scene in heaven concerning the prayers of the saints:

> Then another angel, having a golden censer, came and stood at the altar. He was given much incense, that he should offer it with the prayers of all the saints upon the golden altar which was before the throne. And the smoke of the incense, with the prayers of the saints, ascended before God from the angel's hand.
>
> Revelation 8:3-4, NKJV

Here we see the collective prayers of the saints being mixed with a sweet-smelling fragrance being offered up before the Lord of Glory. This is just to emphasize that our prayers are very precious to God. These fervent prayers permeate the atmosphere of heaven's throne and are before God's presence. As Christians, we can never stop praying. It is our responsibility to be the intercessors for our great nation! More on this later.

The third step is having a thirst and hunger after God. So many people want the blessing of God without the relationship with God. Many approach God always looking for a handout or some type of material blessing. However, God wants us to love Him, with all of our heart, mind, and strength. If He never blesses you with money, power, fame, or influence, the redeemed should be rejoicing in the fact that He sent Jesus to die on the Cross for you. You should be praising God that your name is written in the Lamb's Book of Life. Salvation is the greatest gift God could have given humanity. In Paul's appeal to the Romans, he reasons, "He that spared not his own Son, but delivered him up for us all, how shall he not with him also freely give us all things?" (Romans 8:32, KJV) All we have to do is "...seek ye first the kingdom of God, and his righteousness; and all these things shall be added unto you" (Matthew 6:33, KJV).

Materialism is a problem that festers in our capitalist society. If it is an American problem, then it's an American Church problem, too. Whatever problems exist in society are also problems that will exist in the Church, because people come to the church from society. This is why the American Church suffers from the effects of materialism. However, if it is true that we should all be rich, then we will become a "Laodicean church." It was this church that boasted, "I am rich, and increased with goods, and have need of nothing; and knowest not that thou art wretched, and miserable, and poor, and blind, and naked." The Lord's rebuke of that church was that they were lukewarm. Therefore, He said, "I will spew you out of my mouth." Being "vomited" out of the Lord's mouth does not seem to be an example of God's favor. (See Revelation 3:14-22)

The final step is repentance. Here are the words of the

apostle Paul addressing the Corinthians about repentance:

> Or do you not know that wrongdoers will not inherit the kingdom of God? Do not be deceived: Neither the sexually immoral nor idolaters nor adulterers nor men who have sex with men nor thieves nor the greedy nor drunkards nor slanderers nor swindlers will inherit the kingdom of God. And that is what some of you were. But you were washed, you were sanctified, you were justified in the name of the Lord Jesus Christ and by the Spirit of our God.
>
> 1 Corinthians 6:9-11, NIV 2011

Repentance means a change of heart, mind, and to go in the opposite direction. No matter what bondage you are in, you can repent and come out of it. Many argue that they cannot change because of attributes with which they were born. There is truth to that in this regard: we are all born in sin and shaped in iniquity. The sinful nature that all human beings are born with is desperately wicked and capable of producing all sorts of evil, but that still doesn't mean you cannot repent. Obviously, in the Corinthian church, there were those who were delivered from homosexuality and other sins because Paul said, "and such were some of you." The remedy, "But you were washed, you were sanctified, you were justified in the name of the Lord Jesus Christ and by the Spirit of our God." This is the essence of repentance.

When the people of God are right with the Lord, then they can stand in the gap for this nation. Therefore, "if my people, who are called by my name, will humble themselves and pray and seek my face and turn from their wicked ways, then I will hear from heaven, and I will forgive their sin and will heal their land."

The Curse of Esau

In chapter one, we examined how Esau sold his birthright and lost his blessing to his brother Jacob. The pertinent question is, what caused Esau to make these terrible decisions? The answer is that he had no respect for the things or the people of God. Thus, this is the legacy of Esau. In Hebrews, we get a glimpse of Esau from a New Testament perspective. Hebrews informs us:

> Make sure that no one is immoral or godless like Esau, who traded his birthright as the firstborn son for a single meal. You know that afterward, when he wanted his father's blessing, he was rejected. It was too late for repentance, even though he begged with bitter tears.
>
> Hebrews 12:16-17, NLT

Here Esau is classified as *immoral* and *godless*, a legacy that was passed to his descendants the Edomites. How do you think God would classify America? As righteous and holy? Any people or a nation in situations similar to the Edomites live under a perpetual curse and repetitive calamity and do not have the favor of God abiding over them. Esau had a wicked heart, which was manifested in that he cared nothing for the things pertaining to God, nor cared anything for the people of God. Therefore, the litmus test of whether a nation can or is allowed to repent will be determined on how that nation treats the things pertaining to God, and even more specifically, how it treats the saints who are called by God's name.

As we have covered in this book, America is a land that is rich in natural resources, so much so that it America has become one of the greatest industrial powers the world has ever known. However, America is not only rich in natural resources, but she is also rich in spiritual resources. Though iniquity does abound, this country has the benefit of millions of Christians that live and practice in the United States. We are the people who are called by God's name. Our fervent and effectual prayers can avail much. If left to herself, America is headed for certain destruction, so we need to do what God has called us to do, because we are the "Church of the living God, the pillar and the ground of truth." God can delay judgment on America on our behalf. However, America, be forewarned: it is how you treat God's people that will determine your outcome. This is a clarion call for the churches of Jesus Christ to put our differences aside, and come to the unity of the faith, to intercede for our great nation that she will find true repentance.

Turn this Nation Around!

"...but the people who know their God shall be strong, and carry out *great exploits*. And those of the people who understand shall instruct many..."
Daniel 11:32-33, NKJV

In Matthew 16:18, Jesus makes this declaration, "...I will build my church; and the gates of hell shall not prevail against it." This is all we need to know. Jesus has emphatically stated that the kingdom of darkness and the kingdoms of this world cannot, and will not, prevail against the Church. We already have the victory. Similarly, John writes: "...and this is the victory that overcometh the world, *even* our faith (1 John 5:4, KJV). Therefore, we need to use what we have at our disposal to do great exploits for the kingdom of God. As Christians, we need to be on fire, telling everyone we can about the Lord's saving grace.

My appeal to all of the great Christian leaders of this nation, to all those who have the huge mega-conferences, all of the mega-churches throughout this great country, instead of having conferences that focus on wealth and prosperity, self-improvement, reaching your destiny, claiming your blessing and such, put those agendas aside and have conferences where the theme is "turn this nation around." The preachers with the mega-platforms should start inciting an army of Christian soldiers to get off of the benches and become active in society, and to be the lights of the world that the Lord called us to be. We should not be the bystanders or complainers, but the doers, movers and shakers that are willing to do exploits that will bring glory to God. Forget separation of church and state. In Jeremiah, the Bible teaches that believers should be involved in the betterment of their societies. "And work for the peace and prosperity of the city where I sent you into exile. Pray to the Lord for it, for its welfare will determine your welfare" (Jeremiah 29:7, NLT). Clearly, God was not telling His people to do nothing while they were in Babylon "as captives." He was saying get busy, get involved, and intercede for the peace and prosperity of your city. We Christians are great with coming together amongst ourselves inside the four walls of the church, but we are disjointed outside the walls of the church. We have to get involved in every sector of society.

Too many Christians do not want to come out of our comfort zones and get involved. For once, can we come to the unity of the faith and stop being tossed around by every wind of denominational difference? Just imagine, if all those people who attended these multinational conferences come together and focus not on themselves or the rock-star preachers, but concentrate on appealing to God to heal our land, then we could turn this nation around. As Christian soldiers numbering in the tens of thousands and millions bombarding heaven with our prayers and repentance, we can take back what the devil has stolen from us. However, too many Christians are too distracted with using "the faith" to obtain material blessings for themselves. This is why Jesus taught seek ye first the kingdom of God, and all the things will be added. There is a bigger, more important agenda with which to be concerned.

Today you hear it predicted by many that there will be a great end-time revival. I certainly believe that this is true, but it's going to come at a cost. The Bible teaches that "all who desire to live godly in Christ Jesus will suffer persecution" (2 Timothy 3:12). However, the first spark igniting this revival is when the saints of the Most High God call out to God to turn this nation around. If we can get to the place where the Church raises up its voice and cries out against this nation's wickedness, despite the consequences and despite the persecution, God will do mighty exploits. God does great, miraculous exploits in the milieu of adversity. Think about it, mostly all of the miraculous exploits recorded in the Scriptures happen at times of distress, challenge, adversity, or need. When the darkness arises, and wickedness increases, this is when the light of the saints shines the brightest.

In Acts 8:1, Luke records "…And at that time there was a great persecution against the church which was at Jerusalem; and they were all scattered abroad…" (Acts 8:1, KJV). The *Tyndale Commentary* gives us some insight into how persecution contributed to the spreading of the gospel, which I believe will be the underpinning of this next great revival. "The scattering of the Christians led to the most significant step forward in the mission of the church. One might say that it required persecution to make them fulfill the implicit command in Acts 1:8,"[73] (…and ye shall be witnesses unto me both in Jerusalem, and in all Judaea, and in Samaria, and unto the uttermost part of the earth).

Finally, though iniquity may abound, and wickedness may increase, the darkness cannot overpower the glorious light of the gospel of Jesus Christ. America cannot be delivered by military might, economic empowerment, or political power, but by God's Spirit. Her deliverance can only come by way of national repentance. Let all who name the name of Jesus be on one accord and pray that we can turn this nation around for the betterment of our beloved country. It is my hope and prayer that God does bless America. May the grace and faith of our Lord and Savior Jesus Christ be with you always. Amen.

The End

About the Author

Dr. Dennis J. Woods has studied eschatology for 40 years. His fascination with biblical prophecy began in 1975 while serving in the Navy on board the *U.S.S. England*, after reading his first Hal Lindsey book. In 1982, after being honorably discharged, he continued his eschatological studies, reading great dispensational teachers such as Clarence Larkin's books *Dispensational Truth, the Book of Revelation* and *Daniel.*

In 1994, Dr. Woods' first book, *Unlocking the Door: A Key to Biblical Prophecy*, was published, giving him national exposure. In 1995, he further sharpened his eschatological skills by taking a Revelation course taught by renowned New Testament theologian Dr. D.A. Carson at Trinity Evangelical Divinity School, Wisconsin extension, Elm Brook Church, where Dr. Steward Briscoe was pastor. In 1997, he also corresponded with Dallas Theological Seminary pillars Dr. John Walvoord (2004) and J. Dwight Pentecost (2014).

Today, Dr. Woods is President and CEO of Life To Legacy, LLC, a thriving independent book publisher that has published over 40 titles. He is also the pastor of Power of the Holy Ghost Deliverance Ministries, having nursing home and radio outreach ministries in Chicago, Illinois. For their spiritual enrichment, he and his wife of 18 years, Chantia, attend the Apostolic Church of God, in Chicago, Illinois, where Dr. Byron T. Brazier is the pastor. In 2004, Dr. Woods received his Doctorate of Biblical Studies from the Midwest Theological Institute of Indiana.

All speaking engagement requests for the author should be submitted to:

Life2legacybooks@att.net

Endnotes

Introduction

[1]Marshall E. Hatch, Prelude to Project America: Memoirs of Faith & Hope To Win the Future, (IL: Life to Legacy, LLC, 2012), p. vii.

Chapter 1

[2]David L. Cooper, The God of Israel, (Biblical Research Society, Abridged ed., 1973), p. iii.

[3]John F. Walvoord and Roy B. Zuck, eds., The Bible Knowledge Commentary: Old Testament, (IL: Victor Books, 1985), p. 1370.

Chapter 2

[4]Hastings' Dictionary of the Bible, ed. James Hastings, reprint ed. (MI: Baker Books, 1994), Obadiah, p. 577.

[5]James Strong, Strong's Exhaustive Concordance of the Bible "Hebrew Chaldee Dictionary," (TN: Thomas Nelson Publishers,1990), ref.5662.

[6]Merrill C. Tenney, The Zondervan Pictorial Encyclopedia of the Bible, Vol. 4, (MI: Zondervan, 1975), p. 480.

[7] The Zondervan Pictorial Encyclopedia of the Bible, vol. 2, p. 342.

[8] Derek Kidner, Tyndale Old Testament Commentaries – Genesis, (IL: InterVarsity Press Academic, 2008)

[9] Strong, "Hebrew Chaldee Dictionary," ref. 3290.

[10] Strong, "Hebrew Chaldee Dictionary," ref. 959.

[11]The Bible Knowledge Commentary: Old Testament,

p. 1454, Obadiah

[12]The Zondervan Pictorial Encyclopedia of the Bible, vol. 2, pp. 201-202

[13]Ibid.

[14]Ibid.

[15]Ibid., p. 204.

[16]Flavius Josephus, Jewish Antiquities XIII, ix, 1; XV, vii, 9.

[17] Tyndale Old Testament Commentaries – Proverbs/ Psalms

[18]Tyndale Old Testament Commentaries – Obadiah, Jonah and Micah

[19]Strong, "Hebrew Chaldee Dictionary," ref. 8487.

[20]The Bible Knowledge Commentary: Old Testament, p. 1456.

[21]Strong, "Hebrew Chaldee Dictionary," ref. 894.

[22]John F. MacArthur, The MacArthur New Testament Commentary: Revelation 1-11, (IL: Moody Publishers, 1999).

CHAPTER 3

[23] "Roots of the U.S.-Israel Relationship." Accessed September 4, 2015. Jewish Virtual Library, http://www.jewishvirtuallibrary.org/jsource/US-Israel/roots_of_US-Israel.html.

[24] Ibid

[25] Ibid

[26] Ibid

[27] Ibid

[28] Ibid

[29] Ibid

[30] Ibid

[31] Ibid

[32] Ibid

[33] Ibid

[34] Ibid

[35] Ibid

[36] Ibid

[37] Ibid

[38] "Israel." Accessed September 04, 2015. U.S. Department of State, http://www.state.gov/r/pa/ei/bgn/3581.htm.

Chapter 4

[39] Bill Chappel, "U.S. Students Slide in Global Ranking On Math, Reading, Science," NPR, December 3, 2013, accessed September 4, 2015. http://www.npr.org/sections/thetwo-way/2013/12/03/248329823/u-s-high-school-students-slide-in-math-reading-science.

[40] The Internet Movie Database; IMDb; IMDb's page for The Devil Wears Prada, accessed September 26,2015,http://www.imdb.com/title/tt0458352/trivia?tab=qt&ref_=tt_trv_qu.

[41] Tyndale Old Testament Commentary – Isaiah, p. 64.

[42] We Just Decided To," an episode in The Newsroom, Season 1, Episode 1, HBO Entertainment; The

Internet Movie Database; IMDb, accessed September 26, 2015,http://www.imdb.com/title/tt2289479/trivia?tab=qt&ref_=tt_trv_qu.

[43] http://www.deathpenaltyinfo.org/innocence-list-those-freed-death-row

[44] Shawna Thomas, "Obama draws 'red line' for Syria on chemical and biological weapons," NBC News, August 20, 2012, http://firstread.nbcnews.com/_news/2012/08/20/13379062-obama-draws-red-line-for-syria-on-chemical-and-biological-weapons.

Chapter 5

[45] http://www.nytimes.com/1991/12/28/world/philippines-orders-us-to-leave-strategic-navy-base-at-subic-bay.html?pagewanted=all

[46] Senate Committee Report on Drugs, Law Enforcement and Foreign Policy chaired by Senator John F. Kerry. Subcommittee on Terrorism, Narcotics and International Operations of the U. S. Senate Committee on Foreign Relations (April 1989). p. 86. Retrieved April 25, 2015.

[47] Nicolas J.S. Davies, "35 countries where the U.S. has supported fascists, drug lords and terrorists," Salon, March 8, 2014, http://www.salon.com/2014/03/08/35_countries_the_u_s_has_backed_international_crime_partner/.

[48] http://www.theguardian.com/world/2015/oct/03/three-medecins-sans-frontieres-staff-killed-in-afghanistan-hospital-bombing

Chapter 6

[49] Thomas Jefferson. Jefferson's Letter to the Danbury Baptists: The Final Letter, as Sent. The Library of Congress Information Bulletin: June 1998. Library of Congress, June 1998. Web. Aug 7, 2010.

[50] The News Nerd Staff, "Boy Suspended from School For Reading Bible During Recess," The News Nerd, July 1,2015,http://www.thenewsnerd.com/local/boy-suspended-school-reading-bible-recess/.

Chapter 7

[51] Anup Shah, "Poverty Facts and Stats," Global Issues, January 7, 2013, http://www.globalissues.org/article/26/poverty-facts-and-stats.

[52] Jillian Eugenios, "Top countries for billionaires – China," CNN Money, Big Money, June 6, 2014, http://money.cnn.com/gallery/luxury/2014/06/01/top-countries-billionaires/2.html

[53] Dan Berman, "12 Countries With Most Millionaires 2015: World Wealth Report," ThinkAdvisor, June 30, 2015, http://www.thinkadvisor.com/2015/06/30/12-countries-with-most-millionaires-2015-world-wea?page=13

[54] Eric Foner, The Fiery Trial: Abraham Lincoln and American Slavery, (NY: W. W. Norton & Company, 2010), . p. 26.

Chapter 8

[55] Strong, "Hebrew Chaldee Dictionary," ref. 1361.

[56] The NIV Exhaustive Bible Concordence, Hebrew to

English Dictionary-Index ref. 1467

[57] Tyndale Old Testament Commentaries – Daniel, volume 23

[58] American Heritage Dictionary of the English Language. 3rd ed., s.v. "eagle."

[59] Elizabeth Nix, "How did the bald eagle become America's national bird?," History, February 25, 2015, http://www.history.com/news/ask-history/how-did-the-bald-eagle-become-americas-national-bird.

[60] Benjamin Radford, "Why Is the Bald Eagle America's National Bird?," LiveScience, September 13, 2010, http://www.livescience.com/32811-why-is-the-bald-eagle-americas-national-bird-.html.

[61] "American Eagle & Native American Indian," American Eagle Foundation website, accessed September 4, 2015, http://www.eagles.org/programs/eagle-facts/american-indian.php.

CHAPTER 9

[62] The MacArthur New Testament Commentary: Revelation 1-11.

CHAPTER 10

[63] David Hinckley, "Average American watches 5 hours of TV per day, report shows," Daily News, March 5, 2014, http://www.nydailynews.com/life-style/average-american-watches-5-hours-tv-day-article-1.1711954

[64] http://www.heraldnet.com/article/20130112/NEWS02/701129949

[65] http://www.newsweek.com/45th-mass-shooting-america-2015-378803

[66] U.S. Department of State, The Great Seal of the United States, U.S. Department of State Bureau of Public Affairs, July 2013, http://www.state.gov/documents/organization/27807.pdf, p. 6.

[67] Washington's Blog, "America Has Been at War 93% of the Time – 222 out of 239 Years – Since 1776," InfoWars, February 21, 2015, http://www.infowars.com/america-has-been-at-war-93-of-the-time-222-out-of-239-years-since-1776/.

[68] Julia Lurie, "This Map Shows Where America's Gun Owners Are," Mother Jones, July 8, 2015, http://www.motherjones.com/politics/2015/06/gun-owners-study-one-in-three.

[69] Ibid.

Chapter 11

[70] Historic Documents. The Pledge of Allegiance. US History website, accessed September 4, 2015, http://www.ushistory.org/documents/pledge.htm.

[71] Matthew Henry, Matthew Henry Concise Commentary of the Whole Bible, (TN: Thomas Nelson, 2013), Nahum1:1-8.

[72] Tyndale Old Testament Commentaries – 2 Chronicles 7 Introduction.

[73] Tyndale New Testament Commentaries – Acts.

About the Publisher

Let us bring your story to life! With Life to Legacy, we offer the following publishing services: manuscript development, editing, transcription services, ghostwriting, cover design, copyright services, ISBN assignment, worldwide distribution, and eBook production and distribution.

Throughout the entire production process, you maintain control over your project. We also specialize in family history books, so you can leave a written legacy for your children, grandchildren, and others. You put your story in our hands, and we'll bring it to literary life! We have several publishing packages to meet all your publishing needs.

Call us at: 877-267-7477, or you can also send e-mail to: Life2Legacybooks@att.net. Please visit our website:

www.Life2Legacy.com

CPSIA information can be obtained
at www.ICGtesting.com
Printed in the USA
FSOW01n0231290416
19825FS